WORKING GREENER

WORKING GREENER

Sustainable work strategies for organisations, industry and business

Kathleen Ralston
and
Chris Church

First published in 1991 by
Green Print
an imprint of The Merlin Press
10 Malden Road, London NW5 3HR

© Kathleen Ralston 1990, Chris Church 1991

The right of Kathleen Ralston and Chris Church to be identified as authors of this work has been asserted in accordance with the Copyright, Design and Patents Act 1988.

All rights reserved. No part of this publication may be reproduced, stored in a retrieval system, or transmitted, in any form or by any means electronic, mechanical, photocopying, recording or otherwise, without the prior permission in writing of the publisher.

ISBN 1 85425 064 7

Phototypeset by Computerset Ltd., Harmondsworth, Middlesex

Printed in England by Biddles Ltd., Guildford, Surrey on recycled paper.

CONTENTS

Author's notes	vi
Introduction: A new way of working	1

Part A: MOVING PEOPLE TO ACTION — 9

1	Individuals taking responsibility	11
2	Forming a Sustainable Work Action Group	19
3	Coordinating a Sustainable Work Action Group	29

Part B: WORKING IN SUSTAINABLE WAYS — 39

4	Applying the 3 Rs: Reduce, Reuse and Recycle	41
5	Using paper as if trees mattered	49
6	Energy for working	59
7	Energy-efficient buildings	71
8	Transporting people and products	79
9	Recovering, converting and disposing of waste	87
10	Developing green products, processes and services	95

Part C: MOVING FORWARD — 105

11	Audits, reviews and assessments	107
12	Writing a strategy document	115
13	Going forward informed	119
14	Positive action for the future	127
15	Actions for every workplace	135

Appendix 1	Further reading	141
Appendix 2	Ten ways to save on packaging	145
Appendix 3	Ten steps to a greener office	147

AUTHOR'S NOTES

This edition of *Working Greener* is based on the first edition originally published in Australia and written by Kathleen Ralston. The British edition could not have proceeded without her support.

Special thanks are due to Jan McHarry for work on five chapters and extensive support and information.

In addition this book has benefited enormously from advice, assistance and support from many people including Richard Adams, Angie Barst, Robin Bines, Christopher Bowers, John Button, Fiona Byrne, Cathryn Ferguson, Paul Hackett, Roger Higman, Sheila McCabe, Ed Posey, David Owen, Steve Robinson, Nick Rowcliffe, Pamela Shimmell, John Talbot.

I am also grateful to Jon Carpenter at Green Print for getting the project moving.

Many organisations, large and small, are mentioned in this book. Some have been criticised by environmental groups in the past, and some are the targets of active campaigns. My use of any organisation as a case history or as an example should not be taken as an endorsement of that organisation's overall activities.

Lastly, it is clear that 'working greener' is a permanent process and even as the book went to press new ideas were coming in. Any suggestions, examples or feedback will be very gratefully received, and where possible will be incorporated in future editions. You may write to me at P.O. Box 893, London E5 9RU.

Chris Church

A NEW WAY OF WORKING

'The Environment is not a luxury, nor can it be postponed until later.'
GRO HARLEM BRUNDTLAND, Prime Minister of Norway

The last three years have seen remarkable changes. Business leaders have joined environmentalists in expressing concerns about the future of the planet and urging the same actions. They are doing it for different reasons, but the message to industry is the same: 'Go green or go under.'

These three years have seen unprecedented coverage of environmental issues by the media and a major shift in public opinion has taken place. More and more people are now aware of the damage that is being done and are looking to see positive action to change the situation. Public opinion has swung so far towards concern for the environment that enlightened businesses will no longer ignore it.

We are being told by well-respected scientists that the world can no longer withstand the way we pillage its resources and casually discard what we no longer want. Industry is being identified as the main contributor to the damage and is being told it must recognise its ethical responsibility; as part of the problem, industry must become part of the solution.

To develop solutions to the problems and to make them work, we need people who understand the complex relationships between the work we do and the world we live in. We need people who can take our ideas and transform them into positive visionary actions. We need, in a word, leaders: not leaders in the traditional sense who think more about their own political survival and career prospects, but people who are prepared to take a lead by deciding that these issues are critical and should be tackled immediately.

> *'There is now a real recognition that safeguarding the environment is an integrated part of good business practice.'*
> HRH PRINCE CHARLES

Many organisations are already taking action. Some are merely making superficial adjustments to their 'image', but others are setting fine examples with new products, processes or technology that minimise damage to our environment and lay the foundations for long-term improvements.

Throughout this book you will find examples of how all types of organisation are responding to the environmental challenge. The book will, hopefully, help you develop a response within your organisation both to the challenge of immediate environmental concerns and to the long-term challenge facing all of us – the need to build a sustainable future for this planet.

SUSTAINABLE DEVELOPMENT

Businesses are urged and expected to grow: to add value to natural resources, to find new markets, to produce and distribute high value products. The urgent question that must be addressed is quite simple – how can this be done without further harming the environment?

One possible answer lies in the concept of 'sustainable development'. This phrase was introduced by the World Commission on Environment and Development, whose report is better known as the 'Brundtland Report'.[1] That report defined sustainable development as development that 'meets the needs of the present without compromising the ability of future generations to meet their own needs'.

The key message of the Brundtland Report was that it is possible to achieve a path of global economic development without causing irreparable damage to the environment. It has been suggested by David Pearce in his follow-up book *Blueprint for a Green Economy*[2] that we should look to leave to future generations 'a "wealth" inheritance – a stock of knowledge and understanding, a stock of technology, a stock of man-made capital *and* a stock of environmental assets – no less than that inherited by the current generation'.

The concept of sustainable development has been taken up world-wide. The British government response to the Report was positive; the Prime Minister at the time, Margaret Thatcher, personally endorsed the concept of sustainable development. Coming as it did shortly before the rapid upsurge of interest in environmental matters the Report influenced the production of the government's white paper on the environment, *Our Common Inheritance*.

If the overall theme of the Brundtland Report was a linking of environmental protection with ending poverty and encouraging development, one of the key mechanisms for that was the suggestion, developed by David Pearce, that we put a price on our natural resources; that we stop regarding them as 'free goods' and cost them into our products. As he points out, 'By treating the ozone layer as a resource with zero price there was never any incentive to protect it. Its value to human populations and to the global environment in general did not show up anywhere in a balance sheet of profit or loss'. The fast developing field of environmental economics also implies that everything must be costed, including the true costs of disposal, noxious impact or environmental nuisance value.

This approach has been criticised, not least because of the absurdity of trying to devise a real value or price for an area of tropical rainforest. It has been argued both that such values must be largely arbitrary and also that since such global assets are irreplaceable they must therefore be 'priceless'.

While the issue of 'real costs' may be discussed at length a series of new legislative concepts have come into being and are now being applied through Directives from the European Commission or through the 1990 Environmental Protection Act.

Some of these key points are:

- 'The polluter pays' – the idea is that products or services that generate more pollution should be more heavily taxed than others. This was a key feature of the Control of Pollution Act but implementation has been a long and slow process.
- A requirement for environmental impact assessments to be carried out before projects can be approved.
- Tax incentives to stimulate the sales of products with less environmental impact (such as unleaded petrol).
- Integrated pollution control.
- Specific taxes to limit the problem of global warming – a 'carbon tax' on all fossil fuels.
- Tighter powers for control and enforcement of pollution legislation.
- The 'precautionary principle' – the idea that new products or processes should be regarded as hazardous until shown to be otherwise, a reversal of traditional practice.

These measures should achieve two objectives simultaneously. First, the costs of depleting our natural resources or of polluting would be incorporated into market prices. Second, positive incentives would stimulate the introduction of products with the lowest possible environmental impact.

Some businesses have always put environmental concern high on their agenda but over the last two years there have been many indications of changes taking place across all aspects of industry. In 1990 the *Business in the Environment*[5] report, supported by a wide range of major businesses including IBM, British Telecom, Johnson Wax, British Rail, Tesco and ICI, declared that:

> Society's drive for an ever-improving standard of living has led to the abuse of our environment. Industry, in meeting these demands, has created much of the pollution. Now we have to clean up and industry must take the lead in finding solutions to the planet's problems.
>
> Today we are all members of a society which through the politicians, pressure groups, media and consumers has declared that environmental excellence is an essential ingredient for long-term business survival. That is why environmental issues affect every business, from mining to manufacturing, from tourism to textiles.
>
> Inevitably there are costs – but there are opportunities as well. The challenge for business is to understand the pressures, anticipate the changes, identify the opportunities and act accordingly. The winners will be those who manage this process well.
>
> Good environmental practice is good management.

The real test will of course be in the implementation of these policies and statements.

In the meantime, much of industry and business remains confused about the specific changes that will need to be made, unsure about what new regulations should be brought in, what incentives should be offered for environmentally sensitive practices and what guidelines to set down.

However, while these matters are being resolved there is a component so far disregarded, that sits within sustainable development, and which could be initiated by every working person. That component is the work we do, and the way we do it, to produce the goods and services we offer.

Case Study: Gaps in awareness

A survey in 1990 by the Cranfield School of Management of 200 small businesses revealed major gaps in awareness. 49% of those interviewed admitted that they took almost no measures to protect the environment while 81% claimed to produce no pollution of any kind!

A similar survey by the Institute of Directors suggested that manufacturers were more aware of environmental concerns than were service sector companies – twice as many in the former category had someone in the company specifically responsible for environmental matters than in the latter. But overall 25% had still taken no actions to save energy in the company while 49% of directors were unaware of their personal liabilities.

A NEW CONCEPT OF WORK

> Neither love nor hatred of work is inherent in man – for work has no intrinsic meaning. Work may be a mere source of livelihood or the most significant part of one's inner life.
>
> Mills, *White Collar* (1951)

Every business, every workplace exists to produce something, either a service or a product. Hospitals produce health care, factories produce specific products, farmers produce crops and schools produce educational services. They all transform resources into finished goods or services.

During the transformation process we are capable of harming or enhancing ourselves, our organisations or our environment, and all too often we are unaware of this capacity. Workers have been accused of consuming materials with scant regard for their origins and 'spewing them out' as rubbish with blatant disregard for where the products and pollution end up.

Some workers, such as farmers, can see the fruits of their labour or, in many cases, the destruction caused by their labour. They are close to, and can feel and see, the resources they use and the products they produce. They can directly observe how carefully or how carelessly they have used their major resource, their land. All over the world many are now seeing poorer crops, depleted soil, increased salinity and the loss of topsoil. Some are being moved to action and to make beneficial changes.

But most of us live in cities and work in offices, homes, retail outlets or factories. We usually live away from our workplace and need to travel every day to and from it. Seldom do we see where the resources that we use originate. Most of us work on bits of a product and often do not even see the final product. Almost never do we see what happens to the leftovers we regard as waste. Nevertheless we now know the damage that this way of working has caused our world.

It is time that we moved forward towards a new concept of work; one that brings with it integrity for the work itself and which embraces the spirit of sustainable development.

SUSTAINABLE WORK

Sustainable work is work done in such a way that consideration is given to both economic and ecological factors.

The specific aims of sustainable work are to:

1 Create goods or services that are both economically and ecologically enhancing.
2 Organise the production of goods, services and resources in such a way that they harmonise rather than conflict with natural systems.
3 Utilise proven traditional working practices where appropriate.
4 Develop and use new processes and cleaner technologies appropriate to the industry.
5 Create workplaces which are both aesthetically pleasing and resource-efficient.

These are ambitious aims and success will not come easily. But they are achievable if we are committed to the philosophy underpinning them.

In previous decades, economic considerations have taken precedence over environmental ones. We need to redress that balance, and as we make the decisions relating to more sustainable ways of working so the environmental will have to be given precedence in critical issues. In most cases economic consequences will not be negative, since caring for the environment usually requires more intelligent and efficient ways of working which can lead to cost savings.

Those who wish to take a lead on sustainable work practices will often be quoted the supposed 'economic and political realities' and will have to work around, through or over them. But these realities are often transitory, even fickle, and there is every likelihood that those who are prepared to break new ground in environmentally sound work practices will be applauded or funded tomorrow.

WHERE DO WE GO FROM HERE?

Sustainable work is a new concept but one that we are well equipped to handle. We have already learnt much about leadership, people at work, the work itself, and about economics, technology and change. We now need to apply this knowledge to embrace caring for our environment.

> *'Our policy of operating to the highest environmental standard will not maximise profits in the short term. We are convinced, however, that this policy will lead to considerable long-term advantages in many ways.'*
> Chairman's message in the Caird Group *Annual Report* (1990)

As with any major change, we are unsure what form it will finally take. As we learn more about the effects of our work practices on the environment we will need to revise our strategies, abandoning some and bringing in others. One thing we can be sure of – we will make mistakes before we get it right. But we will know that we are heading in the right direction.

Our need for sustainable work offers us the opportunity to develop new processes, new practices and new products. It is an area of work where those with vision, commitment and inspiration can take a lead. The knowledge that we gain will be our 'intellectual property' and can be spread around a world that desperately needs new ways of working. Sustainable work offers any organisation a chance to take positive action, initially locally and possibly globally.

THE AIM OF THIS BOOK

This book aims to give shape, direction and suggestions for actions to achieve sustainable work practices in our workplaces and to make those actions available and relevant to anyone who wants to take the first steps.

Part A discusses 'Moving people to action' and offers suggestions to people on how to start to bring about new ways of working in their own workplace, either as an individual or by forming a Sustainable Work Action Group (SWAG). The chapter on 'Co-ordinating a sustainable work programme' is specifically for those medium to large organisations who will want to appoint a co-ordinator to implement such a programme: it sets out guidelines and actions for such a person to successfully implement the changes needed.

Part B looks at the changes to be made to products and practices to achieve the aims of sustainable work. It recognises that before people will willingly change to new ways of working they need to know *why* they are being asked to change and given guidelines on *how* to change.

Consequently these chapters include:

- information on a particular environmental issue that is creating the need to change.
- actions that have been taken worldwide or in the UK to rectify the problem.
- guidelines and suggested actions to help people work more effectively with the particular resource or material.

Throughout the book there are case studies and examples of how other workplaces in Britain and elsewhere are handling each issue. It is hoped that these examples may trigger off some ideas on how you can work in more sustainable ways in your own workplace.

In Part C all the ideas are linked into 'Moving forward'. It looks at producing a sustainable work strategy for your organisation and how you might get it accepted and implemented. It examines the role of audits and assessments and looks at companies moving beyond those guidelines. There is also a comprehensive list of the bodies, guides and other books that are available to provide further support and information.

If we are to achieve a balance between our industrial and natural world we have to work in new ways. There are signs of change everywhere but there must be more impetus and more people willing to lead the way by taking up the challenge in individual workplaces. This book aims to give that impetus. We hope that it will move you to action.

NOTES

1 The 'Brundtland Report' is published as *Our Common Future*, Oxford University Press, 1987 (ISBN 019 282 080 X).
2 *Blueprint for a Green Economy*, by David Pearce *et al.*, Earthscan Books, 1989 (ISBN 1 85383 066 6).
3 *Your Business and the Environment* is published by Business in the Environment, price £5. See 'Further reading'.

PART A

MOVING PEOPLE TO ACTION

'The greatest problem we face in the world today is not the myriad of environmental problems, not economics, not hunger, not nuclear weapons.

The biggest problem is to move people to action.'

JOHN DENVER, singer and conservationist

CHAPTER 1
INDIVIDUALS TAKING RESPONSIBILITY

'The environment is the business of everybody, development is the business of everybody, life and living is the business of everybody.'
                    JOSEPH OUMA, Dean of the School of Environment Studies,
                    Moi University

During the last few years people have come to realise the damage that industrialisation has caused and is causing to our world. Sometimes the damage is obvious – pollution of our rivers and beaches or air pollution in our cities – but other damage is more insidious. We cannot feel the 'effect' of the 'greenhouse' and we cannot see the depletion of the ozone layer. But we are now convinced that they are occurring and will get worse unless we do something to change our ways of living and working.

Industry has both the challenge and the opportunity to lead the way in these changes, for the business world now has influence that it never had before. Business leaders are increasingly asked to comment on a myriad of issues. Their opinions are listened to and acted upon and they affect our political systems, our community welfare, our research and development and our higher education.

This may or may not be desirable; it all depends on what they value and what they see as excellence. Unfortunately, all too often excellence is equated with profit, size, and growth. The businesses that get praised are those who grow fastest and who make major short-term gains. The cover stories on business magazines feature 'The top earners – who they are and what they are worth' or 'A comprehensive guide to the size, growth and performance of Britain's biggest businesses'.

Of course organisations must make a profit. Of course excellence should be applauded. But the critical questions are – profit from what? The best in what? Cannot the profit come from being the best at developing in sustainable ways? It is time for industry to develop different ways of measuring excellence. For a sustainable future, excellence must be about the quality and durability and ultimate recyclability of the things that we produce; efficiency in use of resources; creativity in developing new clean technologies and vigilance in reducing and disposing of unrecyclable waste.

When we see the business magazines acclaiming:

'Our top 100 conserver companies'
'The UK's most energy-efficient companies'
'The best of the environmental innovators'
'Our finest waste reducers'
'Our 100 outstanding innovations for sustainable development'

then we will know that industry has accepted the moral responsibility for leading the way towards a sustainable future.

It is of course not enough just to look to industry. The public sector has a key role to play in bringing about this change. Local authorities are the guardians of our local environment and need to be encouraged to integrate environmental concern into all aspects of their work and planning. Civil servants must play a key role in ensuring the implementation of new regulatory measures and legislation. And above all, the educational system has a responsibility to teach and train young people to think about working and living sustainably throughout their lives.

TAKING RESPONSIBILITY

When chief executives or the managers of small businesses decide to move towards more sustainable ways of working, the change may be surprisingly easy. Their values will filter down the organisation and, if the values are shared by the staff, they will provide a sense of 'knowing where we are going', a guideline for day-to-day behaviour.

New products, new practices and processes, no matter how much they are needed or how brilliant is their concept, will only happen and succeed if someone takes responsibility for them. That may be the chief executive but more often a chief executive will not take on that role.

It is far more likely that the first to agitate for new ways of working will be the young, not least because it is their future at stake. But young people

> *'Responsibility, which is sometimes glorious, is often terrifying. But without it one is nothing.'*
> SHIRLEY HAZZARD, 1984 Boyer Lectures

tend to be low in the organisational hierarchy. Given half a chance these people would be eager to take up the challenge that our economic and environmental chaos is creating. For the sake of the future of both ourselves and our organisations, senior management must give them that 'half a chance'.

Those at the top and middle of organisations need to put out signals to staff that they are open to suggestions on 'greening' the organisation. They should be constantly alert for staff who show a commitment to sustainable work and keep the avenues of communication open for those staff to approach them. These ideas should not be seen as 'oddball suggestions from junior staff' but as positive contributions to developing the future of the organisation.

Staff at the lower levels in large organisations should not wait for that 'half a chance' to be formally offered them but should let their managers know of the ideas that they have and their willingness to work on them. Saving the planet cannot 'wait for later': the job is urgent and people who have ideas and energy are precious resources who should be supported and encouraged.

Ultimately it does not matter how 'senior' or 'junior' you are. The simple fact that you have a job gives you the power to make a difference in your workplace: every worker has the responsibility and the opportunity to move their organisation towards more sustainable ways of working.

'WHAT, ME HELP SAVE THE PLANET?'

As we said, every worker can do something. Listed below are just some ideas about how some workers can take positive action.

Accountants and **economists** can:
- devise practical ways to assist companies to measure environmental improvements which would justify cleaner technology and result in higher long-term returns.
- develop new macro-economic 'tools' to assess the implications of environmental degradation for society.
- develop tools that can assist business to build in costs of previous 'free goods'.
- use their skills as analysts to help develop realistic reporting methods for environmental review processes.

Architects can:
- suggest to clients that they should not build commercial buildings for today, but for 10 or 20 years ahead, so that their buildings will be energy efficient and so more attractive in a highly-competitive market.
- suggest passive energy designs as an integral aspect of any new commercial or industrial building.
- point out the long-term benefits of such buildings to both the users and society.
- review their specifications and avoid using tropical hardwoods or environmentally damaging materials in any design.

Builders can:
- ensure that all building work incorporates as much insulation material as possible.
- ensure that construction practices are planned so as to minimise pollution on and off site.
- recycle timber and other materials from older buildings where appropriate.

Cleaning staff can:
- ensure that they only use products with minimum environmental impact.
- reduce the use of such unnecessary products such as air fresheners and toilet water colourers.
- organise night-time cleaning teams so that minimum lighting is used as they move around large buildings.

Commercial kitchen staff can:
- ensure training of all staff in energy efficiency.
- set up recycling programmes for paper, glass, aluminium and organic matter for composting.
- review their purchasing policy regularly and attempt to use local produce where possible.
- consider offering and promoting organic food dishes as a 'high-quality' alternative.

Council staff and councillors can:
- set up and run their own council buildings as models of good practice for residents and businesses to follow.
- establish and operate systems to ensure freedom of information regarding council policies.
- ensure that new or re-designed buildings use passive energy sources.
- set maximum standards for energy efficiency in all new building work.

- establish recycling programmes in all council buildings.
- set progressive targets for all residential waste recycling schemes.
- integrate new measures to control litter with a policy of waste reduction.
- involve local businesses in litter and waste reduction schemes.
- insist on best practice in all waste management schemes.
- train all senior staff in environmental awareness and encourage them to take a lead in setting up departmental sustainable work plans.
- choose fuel-efficient vehicles for council work and ensure they are well maintained.
- end the use of all pesticides that have been shown to cause environmental hazards and look to develop the 'organic' management of parks and open spaces.
- support local voluntary environmental and development groups.
- develop traffic calming and control measures in residential areas and introduce cycle routes and car-free zones.
- act as a focus for environmental concern by all sections of the community.

Designers can:
- use minimum resources in any design.
- specify products that minimise the environmental impact of any design.

Engineers can:
- inform and persuade clients of the importance of environmental issues when planning new developments.
- incorporate environmental assessment and audits in all new projects.
- insist on environmental protection whilst building new projects.

Entertainment industry staff can:
- suggest that events are not held where they will damage the environment.
- develop measures for environmental protection at all venues.
- provide facilities such as recycling bins, so that the suggested practices can be carried out.
- provide support and expertise for fund-raising and awareness events for environment and development groups.

Factory staff can:
- question the use of any toxic substances and hazardous materials.
- suggest the use of other materials with less environmental impact.
- set up recycling and re-use programmes.

- assess the working processes that are used and suggest more sustainable practices.

Gardeners can:
- avoid the use of peat-based composts.
- use organic fertilisers and pest-control methods.

Governments can:
- institute financial incentives to encourage the use of technologies that cause less pollution and save energy.
- develop regulatory and legislative measures to ensure that environmentally damaging policies are phased out.
- put more resources into those aspects of environmental improvement that need central planning, such as efficient public transport schemes and waste minimisation programmes.
- support international agreements on climate change, protection of forests and endangered species and cutting pollution, and lobby that these agreements be made as strong as possible.
- fund and co-ordinate long-term planning towards sustainable development.

Hairdressers and **Beauty consultants** can:
- stock only products that have minimum environmental impact and have not been tested on animals.
- promote these products to their clients.

Investment advisers can:
- suggest investments in 'green' industries.
- monitor the credentials of companies making green claims.

Managers or **owners of small businesses** can:
- set up sustainable work programmes in their organisations.
- look to produce only products that enhance the environment.
- allocate funds to researching and developing processes that will minimise the company's environmental impact.
- support local or national initiatives by voluntary groups.
- invest only in organisations that have a track record of care for the environment.

Marketing, public relations and **sales people** can:
- ask to see full environmental assessments of any product before promoting it with an environmental strategy.
- avoid meaningless phrases such as 'environmentally friendly'.
- pursue opportunities for products that will genuinely enhance the environment.

- question the ethics of any product or service that they are asked to market.

Media workers can:
- write articles about businesses that applaud the new values of conserving resources.
- search out those companies that are at the 'cutting edge' of environmental improvement.
- give coverage to national and local campaigns to protect and improve the environment.
- give advice to campaign groups on developing a media strategy.

Medical staff can:
- ensure that disposal of hazardous medical waste is done to the highest standards.
- monitor and minimise waste in hospitals.
- influence nationwide policy through bodies such as the Royal College of Nursing or the British Medical Association.
- highlight the links between personal health and a healthy environment.

Office staff can:
- set up and run recycling programmes, especially for office paper.
- ban the use of disposable cups.
- set up an office sustainable work team.
- let other sections know of their work and pass ideas around the organisation (See Appendix 3).

Plumbers can:
- insist on high-quality materials and labour to protect our water supplies.
- act as 'watchdogs' for unsound practices. In Australia a scheme called 'Envirosafe' was set up by the New South Wales government and the Master Plumbers Association to cut pollution caused by illegal plumbing and drainage. Plumbers are encouraged to have a 'soft policing role' under the plan.

Publishers can:
- produce all books and promotional material on recycled paper.
- abolish the use of plastic foams in packaging.
- take an ethical stance on what they do and do not publish in relation to environmental issues.

Purchasing officers can:
- insist on buying locally-made products to cut transport costs and pollution while stimulating the local economy.

- purchase items that are re-usable, repairable and recyclable.
- insist on products with minimum packaging.
- purchase in bulk.
- look for the new 'fair trade mark' when buying from abroad.

Supermarket staff can:
- suggest that more 'green' products are stocked.
- suggest energy saving schemes with refrigeration and lighting.
- help to actively promote 'green' products in the stores.

Teachers can:
- use environmental issues as cross-curricular themes.
- set positive examples to students on environmental issues.
- use the school or college as a model for sustainable work practices.
- provide encouragement to those students who wish to specialise in environmental issues.

Tourist industry staff can:
- promote those tourist companies and services that have active environmental policies.
- encourage travellers to care for the environments on the places they visit.
- promote the 'take nothing but photographs, leave nothing but footprints' approach to natural habitats.

And that's just a start!

Don't forget that everyone who is committed to a more environmentally aware life and workstyle is acting as a teacher and a leader. Simply by working in more sustainable ways, by talking about environmental and development issues, and by suggesting actions to others, you will be taking on an educational role.

You may feel that the actions being taken are not strong enough given the urgency of the problem. You may wish to lobby for stronger measures and get actively involved in the work of local pressure groups. But bear in mind that maintaining those sustainable practices at work is a key part of leading by example. No concerned environmentalist should, for instance, be 'too busy to go to the recycling bank'!

Each time you make a stand against a damaging work practice or lobby for stronger controls you will not only be gaining experience in being assertive about the issues that you believe in, you will also be setting the example for others to follow. People will begin to see that it is *normal* behaviour to be concerned about the environment and this will make it easier for them to change their own behaviour.

CHAPTER 2

FORMING A SUSTAINABLE WORK ACTION GROUP (SWAG)

'Never doubt that a small group of thoughtful committed people working together can change the world. Indeed, it is the only thing that ever has.'

MARGARET MEAD, anthropologist

We can see that there is a great deal that individuals can do to bring about changes – but anyone who has tried will know that, all too often, 'it's just not that easy'. You can change your own ways but as soon as you try and change other peoples' ways of working it becomes far more difficult. Even relatively straightforward plans such as setting up a recycling scheme at work may be seen as 'eccentric' or worse.

You may think you are the only person in your workplace who is worried about the environment. That's probably not the case but often there's only one person prepared to raise the issue at departmental meetings etc. And if that one person is you, then it can be quite a stressful experience. Is the management going to view the ideas as interesting or subversive or too expensive? A report by the Environment Council in 1990 identified people who were prepared to stand up and be counted as 'lone ambassadors' and described the problems some of them face.

Two things have become clear: firstly, it's a lot easier to do almost anything if you've got help, and secondly, there are a lot more 'green' people about than you think – they're just not prepared to stick their necks out.

So, if you think you might be a lone ambassador the first thing is to go out and look for support. There are plenty of ways to spot a potential green co-worker:

- Does anyone ever raise environmental issues during tea or coffee breaks or maybe comment on articles in the papers?

- Has anyone decorated their workspace with environmental pictures or posters?
- Does anyone wear badges, sweatshirts or t-shirts with an environmental theme? Even a World Wide Fund for Nature (WWF) sticker on the car might be a place to start.
- If you are involved in a local environmental or conservation group, find out if another member of the group knows anyone who works in the same place that you do and who might be sympathetic.

The other way forward is to recruit your friends. After all, that's what they're for! Even if there are just two or three of you, that's enough to start planning how you might form your SWAG.

Of course it may be easier than that. You may be a manager or you may be able to talk to a manager who will encourage you to set up the SWAG as an officially recognised group with a coordinator whose time is paid for by the company. Chapter 3 is aimed specifically at those who will manage such a programme.

FORMING YOUR GROUP

If your SWAG is going to work it needs to comprise more than just you and your friends. Like any aspect of work, its success will be measured by others by the quality of the changes it makes and the professional manner in which they are carried out. So you should be looking to recruit people who have abilities in the right areas and are respected in the organisation. It would be ideal also to have representatives from each major area of the organisation that might be affected; e.g. administration, manufacturing, personnel, warehousing, etc. So sit down with your initial friends and think of people you know in these areas who might be your target 'invitees'.

Now think about producing a short note that you could pass to these people when you invite them. In it explain some of the simpler things such a group could examine: recycling office paper, or energy saving, might be places to start. Explain also what the aims of the group are and what time commitment being a member might require. You and your friends should then invite the relevant people to a first meeting. Don't go for too many – six or eight will be enough to start with.

There are other people you might wish to involve in the group, if not at the start, then certainly at a later date. Trade unions have a long history of concern about the working environment and a local branch will know about any major outstanding environmental problems. The TUC has

FORMING A SUSTAINABLE WORK ACTION GROUP (SWAG)

recently produced a manual for all its representatives on environmental matters (See Chapter 13).

If your workplace has a union or unions it is therefore important to involve them, not least because they may have 'sole negotiating rights' with management. If you work with them you will have that as extra support, while if you work in isolation unreceptive management may be able to 'divide and rule' and thus obstruct change. There are also health and safety representatives in most workplaces – they should certainly be asked to contribute to the group in some way. They are also important in the event of any simple review (see below) revealing a serious health problem.

If you think your senior management might be even slightly apprehensive about the group, don't hold the first meeting during working hours but choose a lunch-time session.

THE FIRST MEETING

Like any meeting this first meeting should be planned very carefully, for it could set the tone for future meetings and influence what the group will achieve. Although sustainable work is serious business, there is no reason why the meetings should not be enjoyable occasions to meet with others who are motivated by the same underlying concerns.

Members of the group should be asked beforehand what they would like discussed, and the co-ordinator (that's probably you) should prepare an agenda reflecting those concerns. You should set the scene by giving an initial overview of what the group might want to achieve, possibly giving examples of what other similar organisations have done, and inform members of what actions have already been taken. Allow time for a full discussion, but don't let things drag on. Try and ensure that everyone leaves having agreed to take the next important step.

CONDUCTING A 'WALK-THROUGH REVIEW'

Members of the group may have come up with lots of ideas about how the workplace could be changed, but it is important first to know what is going on *now*.

Ask each SWAG member to conduct their own initial 'walk-through review' (or audit). This is easier than it might sound – they just *walk around* their part of the workplace and take notes. Things to watch out for include:

- equipment left on when not in use.
- lights on when no one is around.

- hissing valves (leaking compressed air or gases) or water leaking from hoses or taps.
- potentially re-usable material being thrown away.

Look for positive points too. Are there any forms of recycling in the organisation? Who set them up? Are there offices where there are signs that people take energy waste very seriously? It could be that this process will turn up new potential members of the SWAG.

Each member should then come back to the next meeting with a brief report from their section. You can all compare notes and will then have a much better overview of the real situation and a good basis from which to plan your programme.

SETTING GOALS AND OBJECTIVES

Once the SWAG members know what is happening in the workplace, they will be ready to set goals. To do this, think as a group about everything that you would like to see happen at work. Yes, everything! Put it all down in one long list and then go through it and make a list of everything that you think *could* happen. Then go through that list and pick out what you want to make happen.

YOUR FIRST GOAL

At this point you should be getting in touch with management, if you are not already. To do that most effectively pick one or two of these targets and think about how you might present them to management. Stress at first that what you're doing is good for the company, both in terms of image and in terms of saving money etc. Think also about how they might respond to your approach.

Take for instance recycling of office paper. They might say, 'Why should we do this?' That's easy to answer. Then they might say, 'It'll never work!' You can answer that one by referring to all those companies where it does work (see Chapter 5). The really sceptical might then say that storing waste paper is a fire hazard or that the firm doesn't have anywhere to store waste paper.

It's at this point where you need to have done your homework. Where is waste currently stored? Who puts it there? When is it taken away? What would the cleaners think about an office recycling scheme? Come up with positive answers to some of these questions and even the most sceptical manager is likely to recognise that you do know what you are talking about.

FORMING A SUSTAINABLE WORK ACTION GROUP (SWAG)

Now is the time to ask them for official support. Can the group now recruit someone from management to attend the meetings, to report back on what is being planned to other managers, and to look for ideas and advice from those other managers? There's probably some rising manager in your organisation who'd like to take on this new responsibility. Ask also if you can take an hour a fortnight for the eight people in the group to meet at work (and to be able to use the photocopier etc). Getting support on this level must be your first goal.

FURTHER GOALS AND OBJECTIVES

Once you've achieved this goal you should now as a group plan your goals for the organisation. Goals should have the following characteristics:

1 be clearly stated and agreed by all members.
2 be of a high standard.
3 be achievable.
4 be measurable.
5 be time-related.
6 be evaluated at appropriate intervals.

Some examples of overall goals for a sustainable work programme might be:

- to achieve a reduction of 20% in energy usage by October 19...
- to be using only recycled paper throughout the organisation by next July.
- to have phased out all uses of CFCs within X years.
- to reduce the consumption of water in the factory by 30% by December 19...
- within X years to be producing only products that are durable, repairable and have minimum environmental impact in their production, use and ultimate disposal.

Setting these goals and gaining agreement will not be easy tasks. But do not rush this phase, for time spent now gaining commitment to a particular course of action will be repaid later on.

Once all goals have been agreed to, then objectives should be set to achieve each of these goals. For example, the objectives for the first goal above could be:

- to check draughtproofing around all doors and windows before November this year.

- to encourage all departments to set up their own energy monitoring system where appropriate.
- to install time switch controls to turn off lights and machinery during the hours when they are not in use.
- to fit lights in the factory and offices with low wattage bulbs.
- to plant 20 strategically placed trees around the site.

PLANNING

Once goals and objectives have been set they will form the basis for planning the actions and the time-frame. Choose one or two of the simplest projects as a place to start and choose ones that have a good chance of being successful and show obvious results. Early successes will not only keep the group enthusiastic but will also begin to favourably influence others within the organisation.

There are some very comprehensive programmes for planning (using ideas such as Critical Path Analysis), some of which come in computer software packages that you may wish to investigate. But for a reasonably simple way forward you can get the group together and:

1 'brain-storm' every action that needs to be taken to achieve one of the goals. This simply involves writing out every idea, in random order, on a board or sheet of paper until no one has any more to offer.
2 put the items into the order in which they will need to be done: e.g. quotes will have to be obtained for new equipment before a report can be sent to management to approve the expenditure.
3 note beside each item the date by which it should be completed.
4 note beside each item who has the responsibility for doing it.

Here is an example:

Action	Date for completion	Person responsible
Contact Section Heads to discuss time switch idea	July 1st	Co-ordinator
Report results to next meeting	July 2nd	Co-ordinator
Arrange quotes for time switches	July 15th	Janet Simpson
Contact tree nursery to arrange visit to select suitable trees	July 15th	Ron Barker

CONDUCTING ACTION MEETINGS

Keeping things moving with the group members will depend very much on the effectiveness of the SWAG meetings. Here are a few pointers for the co-ordinators to ensure that the meetings do lead to positive action.

Before the meeting
Planning before the meeting helps everyone to be focused on exactly what they need to do at the meeting.

- Collect all the relevant information and make a copy available at a central place for all members to read before the meeting (think before you photocopy!) or send to all members via the office electronic mail system if there is one. Talk to members whom you are expecting to report to make sure they know what is expected of them.
- Prepare an agenda, noting the topic item and who is going to be the main speaker. Circulate this if appropriate.
- Indicate the time of starting and how long you expect it will take.
- If you as co-ordinator have a lot to say, ask someone else to take on the duty of chairing the meeting.
- Ensure that someone comes prepared to take notes (this duty and the role of chairing the meeting can be circulated among members).

During the meeting
Use these pointers to ensure that your meetings are action-oriented, conducted efficiently and get results. (Most of these tips are for whoever chairs the meeting.)

- Begin on time!
- Introduce each item clearly so that all members know what is being discussed.
- Keep members to the point of the discussion.
- Be aware of group behaviour and control private discussions and disagreement within the group.
- Face up to the difficult topics and work through them as a group.
- Make decisions on what is to happen, and who is to take the action, before the next meeting. Someone should write these points up on a large sheet of paper that everyone can see so that there is no room for confusion.
- Set the next meeting for a mutually convenient time and agree who will chair it.
- Close the meeting as near as possible to the time suggested on the agenda.

After the meeting
Prepare minutes of the meeting as soon as possible after the meeting, noting in them all agreed points and actions, and especially who is going to do the actions.

GAIN MANAGEMENT APPROVAL FOR ANY PLANNED ACTION

You've got to get your management interested in supporting the group. It is essential that any actions to be taken must all have the support of senior management. For this the SWAG members will need to prepare, very carefully, a management presentation either as a verbal report or in writing.

The aim of this presentation will be two-fold:

1 To persuade senior management of the necessity or advisability of the proposed changes.
2 To persuade them to fund and/or approve the necessary changes.

The following points should be covered in the presentation:
WHY it is necessary to make the change to sustainable work practices.
HOW you intend to make the changes.
WHO will coordinate the changes and who will be affected by them.
WHAT are the advantages and disadvantages of the changes.
HOW MUCH the changes will cost.
WHEN it is anticipated the changes will take place.

Don't forget that you may have to negotiate on some of this, so be aware which parts of your plan are crucial and which are more flexible.

Once you have gained approval, request the senior management to officially advise all staff about the proposed changes and that the SWAG will be organising the changes. This is an absolutely essential part of the programme and must not be overlooked.

IMPLEMENTING CHANGES

Changing the way people work is always a hard and thankless task. Some people will be enthusiastic about your plans, others will ignore them for as long as they can. Look through the next chapter, which has some ideas on how to move forward and choose the ideas that seem most appropriate for your organisation.

Case Study: The power of a group

In July 1989 eight staff members from a large food manufacturing company met voluntarily to 'establish a committee of people interested in reducing wastage.' The group called itself the EMU (Efficient Materials Usage Committee).

Its first action was to investigate the use of materials in members' own particular work areas. Each member took responsibility for a particular material: computer paper, photocopying paper, plastics, metals and wood, glass and aluminium and used oils. Since that date the committee has:

- set up a notice board to invite other staff to join and to display information on relevant environmental items.
- arranged for recycled unbleached paper for internal office use.
- set up various recycling systems around the office, canteen and factory.
- suggested new truck washing procedures.
- investigated fully biodegradable detergents.
- set up a rack of mugs in the canteen in place of plastic disposable ones.
- discussed efficient energy practices with an energy consultant.
- set up discussions with management on the subject of alternative packaging for products.

By the end of its first six months the committee was requested to assist with the development of the company's environmental policy. This included the establishment of an official environmental committee.

CHAPTER 3
CO-ORDINATING A SUSTAINABLE WORK PROGRAMME

'Successfully managing change requires a long-term perspective. This will require that management looks well beyond its own industry to environmental impacts on other industries and on society in general.'
T. D'AQUINO, President, Australian Business Council

Much of the criticism that has been directed at some companies by environmental campaign groups has arisen because it was seen that those companies were attempting to 'greenwash' their products and services. In other words they were making token and superficial attempts to convince the public that they were concerned about the environment when the great majority of their working practices showed the reverse to be true.

It is thus essential that the greening of the organisation that you work for is given policy status and is co-ordinated in just the same way that any other long-term policy development might be. Environmental improvement should be a matter for concern right across the organisation and not just in the PR department. It must therefore become an integral and deep-rooted part of organisation policy.

To make that happen any organisation that commits itself to developing sustainable work practices should appoint a co-ordinator for the programme. In a large organisation that post would be full-time and be similar in standing to that of Health and Safety or Equal Opportunity Officers. In small organisations the role could be assigned, and hours allocated, to any suitable person who is committed to the philosophy of sustainable work.

Once this role has been established, senior management must ensure that the person holding the position receives every possible assistance – by removing political obstacles, by arranging financial assistance and by offering personal support.

A SUSTAINABLE WORK CO-ORDINATOR

Some the duties of a sustainable work co-ordinator would be:

- setting up a Sustainable Work Action Group (SWAG).
- co-ordinating the efforts of the SWAG.
- liaising with senior management.
- liaising with staff and unions.
- acting as researcher/writer for policy/strategy/action documents.
- promoting sustainable work within the organisation and to the general public.
- arranging training programmes in environmental awareness and sustainable work practices.

The qualifications and skills needed by the co-ordinator could include:

- commitment to the philosophy of sustainable work.
- an appropriate qualification.
- a knowledge of environmental and work-related issues relevant to the particular sector.
- ability to work with different levels within the organisation.
- ability to lead and co-ordinate others.
- writing and verbal presentation skills.
- ability to promote the organisation's achievements.

IMPLEMENTING CHANGES

Organisations seldom change unless they are forced to do so by the need to respond to one or both of the following:

1 Pressures, constraints and opportunities from the world outside the organisation.
2 Tension or dissatisfaction expressed by the people within the organisation.

All these factors are operating already in relation to business and the environment. There is a turbulence and energy ready to be captured and channelled into new ideas and working practices. *How* we harness that energy is the crucial factor.

For the co-ordinator of a sustainable work programme, there will be no one 'right' way to bring about the changes. Some strategies will be more appropriate at particular times; different strategies may be equally successful, while some will be effective with one group and not with another. The co-ordinator will need to know a range of strategies and be capable of using them when they seem most appropriate.

THE CONSULTATIVE PROCESS

There is constant change in our workplaces with new technology, new social forces, new demands from the workforce, and we have learnt a lot over the last few years about strategies for successful change. Setting up a sustainable work programme will certainly require major changes and commitment from members of staff and perhaps also from the community. The key is always to involve as many people as possible in both planning and executing the changes so that they feel that they 'own' the new ideas and have a stake in their success.

Implementing a consultative strategy

(1) Form a Sustainable Work Action Group
If carefully selected the members of this group will be an invaluable source of ideas, energy, and support. The co-ordinator should:

- follow the guidelines in the previous chapter to ensure the group works well and remains committed.
- conduct a 'walk through' review (as above).
- follow up with an official 'energy and waste audit' (see relevant chapters). The information gained from these audits will form the basis of the programme.

(2) Inform and educate those affected
Once it has been decided which section or particular work practice will be the first to be handled, let those affected know as soon as possible about the impending change.

First explain the global issues that are creating the need for change and how your organisation or industry can help alleviate the damage. Then explain the particular work practices that are to be changed. Allow time for everyone to ask questions and to express their feelings about the change. This will ensure that all those involved have a deeper understanding of the issues. People who are well informed are far more likely to cope well with change, particularly if they are given plenty of warning and have had their questions sensitively and realistically answered. This period also offers all those involved a chance to contribute initial ideas from their own experience and this will help with the next phase.

'Resistance' is a topic that crops up immediately any mention is made of change. Certainly it is an important aspect of any change process and must be taken into consideration. But it is also often the case that staff are not only ready for the change, they have been wondering why management has taken so long! In most cases it is not the change itself that is resisted but the method used to induce the change.

If you approach the change process with the 'resistance factor' uppermost in your mind, you may be unconsciously setting yourself up for conflict. You may interpret reasonable questioning of your proposal as antagonistic and respond in a defensive or confrontational manner. But if you have been thorough in your preparation of the programme and approach the implementation as an opportunity for everyone to work together towards a better future, you will welcome searching questions.

Questioning is an essential part of any programme of change and should be treated as genuine expression of concern and as a chance to sort out the best way forward together. Without this questioning, many crucial aspects of the programme may be overlooked with disastrous consequences.

(3) Participation and consultation
Sustainable work will affect many aspects of the conditions under which people work and they should have a say in how the change is to come about. By being part of the process and being invited to give their input, they will be more committed to the idea than if it is thrust upon them.

Make sure that you ask people directly for their input. Your questions might include:

- What parts of your job could be more energy-efficient?
- How could you save paper in your section?
- What would you need to change to make use of the waste heat from that machine?
- Is there a less toxic material that we could be using in that process?
- What could your section do to work in ways that are more sustainable?
- How can we best generate favourable coverage for the changes we are making?
- How can we make savings on energy in our car fleet?
- How can we make a similar product that has less environmental impact?

Those who do the work usually have ideas about how to do it better. They may never have been asked before. Given the chance, they will have lots of ideas that you may never have thought of. Make sure their ideas are considered carefully and that the best of them are included in the overall plan.

(4) Plan the strategy
Involve as many people as is reasonable in planning the change process. If your organisation has an annual strategy planning process make the development of an environmental plan a key theme within that. Integrate developing sustainable working practices with all other new development plans. Together plan when and how the changes will take place and set goals for the overall change (see Chapter 2). Then set some short-term targets, so that you can notch up a few 'successfully completed' checkpoints. Remember that enthusiasm for a programme can languish if the end seems too far away!

(5) Sign-post the change
New logos, slogans or posters around the walls and notice-boards will all herald the change. People will get a feeling of anticipation that 'something is happening around here'. They will begin to be psychologically ready for the change.

(6) Take it slow and easy
If people are going to change they need to know *how* to change. Circulate or publicise simple ideas for positive action, linked to the environmental reasons for the change (there are examples throughout this book). These should be ideas that are applicable widely in the organisation. Some will take them up faster than others and in this way the change will start to become part of normal working. People will thus gain knowledge about how sustainable work affects them and begin to know the ideas and jargon that are part of the change. Knowing those words, the jargon, the key phrases is an important part of the 'changing from' and 'changing to' process.

(7) Set up a new 'reward' system
New systems need new 'rewards'. A system should be set up that supports and rewards those who support the change. This could be done formally through the setting of targets and objectives (e.g. a 20% reduction in energy use within the next six months or a 25% cut in wastage by October 30). An informal system could involve the active sponsoring of staff to attend relevant seminars that will assist in the changes. Either way the personal efforts of an individual or group should be watched for, recognised and praised. This could involve a mention in the workplace newsletter or local newspaper or perhaps taking a group to lunch when they have achieved one of their targets.

Competitions could be set up for the 'division with the least waste' or 'section with the best recycling record' and the winners publicly announced. Some companies have already set up annual targets and prizes with a holiday with an environmental theme as a reward for the most motivated individuals.

Don't wait to give rewards until the final goal or a major target has been accomplished. By all means give incentives and celebrate the big wins, but remember that most people want and need more frequent recognition of success – so praise the small achievements along the way.

(8) Keep everyone informed
This can be done in many ways – memos, newsletters, at regular staff meetings, through specially organised meetings, and by making sure that key people personally pass on information through the organisation. Set up a chart of the overall plan on a public notice-board and use stickers to show when each stage of the plan has been successfully completed. Remember that 'every picture is worth a thousand words' and seeing the progress that has been made will help keep commitment high.

(9) Minimise the damage
In the change to sustainable work someone is sure to feel that they are now worse off than they were before. Be quick to listen to complaints and try to minimise the damage that has occurred. The cost and effort of mollifying a disgruntled few will be small compared to that needed to repair the damage if they try to undermine the change process.

(10) Consolidate (and celebrate)
Make sure that everyone knows when some major event in the programme has been completed. Have a launch event; invite staff, customers and local residents to the tree-planting ceremony around the car park; publicly demonstrate the workings of the new energy-efficient heating system. Congratulate *all* those who have been involved. Those who worked on it will be encouraged and rejuvenated and others will be inspired by the evidence of good work. Then keep a close eye on the new system or process and make sure that it does work as well as was intended.

OTHER STRATEGIES

Throughout the programme you may find that other strategies are needed. You may be able to respond more rapidly to a crisis need than by going through a lengthy process of consultation. These ideas should be used in addition to that overall process and not in place of it. Consultation will always be the key.

CHANGE THE ENVIRONMENT ITSELF

Sometimes it is quicker to simply shape the workplace environment to encourage the way that you wish it to change. Just make some simple specific change; you might turn lights off when they are not being used, get your purchasing department to buy a first batch of low-wattage light bulbs to use as replacements in key areas, or simply begin handwriting replies on the bottom of memos. Other people will soon begin to see these as acceptable ways to work and are likely to follow suit. In time, their attitudes may change to match.

STAFF TRAINING AND 'FOLLOW THE LEADER'

We have seen that it is essential that all staff know why the changes are being made, but a key way of making change is to train staff in key areas. A section leader who has been given a more detailed training session on environmental issues will probably be able to return to their own section and do a walk-through review that will produce new ideas for positive change. Similarly, ensuring that technical officers can attend seminars on new developments in their field means that they will be able to help plan the changes in their areas of expertise.

So look to select individuals or small groups to attend training seminars on issues relevant to sustainable work. Some of these could be delivered in-house, possibly by members of the SWAG or by advisers whom they could select. These staff will then go back into the workplace and show others new ideas 'by example'.

This is a good way to bring about change and develop leaders. The proliferation of work-related seminars, workshops and training programmes is evidence that this approach is used extensively in many areas of business and it should work equally well for new sustainable work practices. This strategy works best when the choice of seminar leaders is carried out carefully to ensure that the programme is of a high standard and that the leaders have the ability to explain clearly the topics under debate.

THE PHASED APPROACH

This often works well in circumstances where two different systems can work simultaneously over a transitional period.

One phased approach is to 'time-phase' the change process. Small aspects of the change are brought in throughout the organisation and integrated; some months later the next phase is added and so on until the whole programme is in place. This is an approach that has been used by many organisation running 'no Smoking' campaigns (see below).

Another type of phased approach is to bring the full programme in area by area. For example, one department or building is selected to pioneer the whole environmental programme. When it is established, another section undergoes the change, until the whole organisation has moved to the new way. This approach works best if the first group selected is already sympathetic to the ideas behind the change. They will probably be quite willing to help iron out many of the snags before other groups are asked to change. The change becomes easier for more reluctant groups as they see from the first group that the 'worst case' worries do not materialise. In fact, you may find that those who have been left behind become eager, or even begin themselves, to work in more sustainable ways.

BLOCKING THE OLD WAY

This is simple and direct – advise all staff that the old way of doing things is no longer allowed. This is an effective approach when it is not possible to have two systems working simultaneously or when a change needs to be brought about quickly, such as the phasing out of CFCs as fillers in aerosols.

To be effective, and to cause the least amount of disruption and resentment, the change-over should be *simple* to understand, *reasons* should be given for the change and a *specific date* should be established for the change-over. Unless it is critical that the change be brought about immediately, the longer the period of the advance warning the better, for by the time the change-over occurs it is often already acceptable.

REMAINING POSITIVE

No matter how well you plan, learn, consult and minimise damage you will not be able to account for every contingency that might occur.

Remaining optimistic about the change will sometimes be difficult, but keep in mind that change is a process, not an event. It has taken us since the Industrial Revolution – if not before – to get ourselves into this mess, and we won't get out of it overnight. The changes that are needed to protect and repair the ecosystems of the planet that we all live on will have to come at every level from the domestic to the international. That doesn't give any of us an excuse to sit on the sidelines and wait for others to start their changes:

rather it is essential that those who can see the need for action lead by example and actively lobby and encourage others to take action similarly.

To achieve a major change like this will take perseverance in the face of inevitable set-backs. Perseverance will mean only abandoning goals if they are no longer important – never because they are too tough. The support of other staff, especially those within the SWAG, can be a valuable asset – but most important of all is a clear vision of where you want to be. Hang on to that and getting there can be easier than you think.

Case Study:
Different strategies for implementing a 'no smoking' policy

PHASED APPROACH

Phase 1 A questionnaire was sent to all staff to establish their views on smoking at work with an attached memo explaining why the questionnaire had been issued. Staff were later advised of the results of the questionnaire and the official policy that was being developed from it.

During the year smoking was banned in all conference rooms and washrooms. Cigarette vending machines were removed from all premises. 'Thank you for not smoking' notices were distributed to all staff wishing to place them in their work area.

Phase 2 The following year all offices were officially designated as 'no smoking' areas (unless *all* staff members in a particular office agreed to let smoking continue). All smokers wishing to stop smoking were offered paid leave to attend 'stop smoking' courses.

Staff were kept informed through the staff newsletter of educational items about smoking and about what was happening in their own workplace.

Phase 3 The following year smoking was banned on all premises.

'BLOCKING THE OLD WAY' APPROACH

In October a memo was sent to all staff advising them that all premises would become 'no smoking' areas on July 1st in the following year and that any staff members who attended officially recognised 'stop smoking' courses before that time would have their costs reimbursed.

July 1st following year – smoking banned on all premises.

PART B

WORKING IN SUSTAINABLE WAYS

'Now. Or never.'

HENRY THOREAU

CHAPTER 4

APPLYING THE 3 Rs – REDUCE, REUSE AND RECYCLE

'In the sustainable economy of 2030, the principal source of materials for industry will be recycled goods . . . Industries will feed largely on what is already within the system, turning to virgin raw materials only to replace any losses in use and recycling.'
STATE OF THE WORLD, 1990, (Worldwatch Institute)

To achieve the first two aims of sustainable work, we must:

- create goods that are both economically and ecologically enhancing.
- organise the production of goods and services and the management of resources so they harmonise, rather than conflict, with natural systems.

Everyone within an organisation must be aware of and take some responsibility for the potential environmental impact of their activities. Manufacturing goods or providing services can use or create toxic substances as well as other material that has to be disposed of.

If we are to aim for Total Environmental Quality (TEQ) we need to see best practice within the workplace. This must include rethinking how and why certain products are used. Positive choices need to be exerted. Choose materials and production techniques that create minimum waste and minimum pollution in their eventual disposal. Rethink the design of products to make them easier to reuse or recycle. The 3 R's – *Reduce, Reuse* and *Recycle* – are fundamental to the success of sustainable work:

1 *Reduce* the amount of non-essential products we produce and *reduce* the substances that go into our products or practices that have the potential to become waste.

2 *Reuse* as many materials and products as possible. Make products that can be repaired or reused easily.
3 *Recycle* material that cannot be reused in its original form. Collect items that could be recycled by external contractors. Help create markets for recycled goods by using them in your workplace. If materials recovery is not possible, support energy-from-waste schemes.

REDUCE

Avoiding the creation of waste must be the first step. But all workplace activities have some environmental impact (as does all human activity). Think about how you could reduce the amount and number of different products you use or produce. Can items be repaired or reused?

For every product you make, the question should be asked: 'Is there a *real* need for this product?'

For every material you use, ask: 'Is there a better material that could be used?'

For every process you use, ask: 'Is there a more efficient production method or machine which would minimise the amount of energy or material we use?'

Suggestions for tackling these topics are covered in subsequent chapters.

Reducing energy and resources can save your company money as well as helping the environment. Energy bills will be lower, waste disposal costs can be reduced and your company can gain a positive image in the eyes of staff, shareholders and clients.

Did You Know?

In 1989, a German survey found that Britain was the second biggest producer of waste in western Europe after the Federal Republic of Germany. However while Germany recycled half the waste it produced, Britain only managed to sort or compost 5%. The survey found that Denmark was the best country for recycling. Only 12% of household waste went to landfill, compared with 90% in Britain.

REUSE

For every product or piece of waste created within the workplace you need to ask: 'Is there a way this could be reused or recycled by us or by someone else?'

Design for reuse or recycling is an important issue. If you manufacture goods, try to limit the number of different materials used in the product. Avoid combinations that make reuse or separation for recycling impossible. Make products that can be dismantled for easy maintenance and repair.

There are thousands of items that we can use and throw away in our workplaces that could be cleaned and reused with no detriment to health and safety. Medical personnel are now reassessing the 'throwaway mentality' that is prevalent in the medical field. They are questioning whether all the items that are used just once and then thrown away, really do need to be discarded. Some could be sterilised for reuse. So if the healthcare profession can reuse materials and products, there is no reason why offices, factories, and shops can't do the same.

Look around your workplace with this in mind. If items are broken yet mendable, arrange for repairs to be carried out. If items need cleaning, see that it gets done. Ensure that you have a regular servicing contract if you hire machinery. Don't discard items if there is still some use left in them. If you can't use them, find someone you can. If appropriate, donate items like old desks and typewriters to a local charity. Before you needlessly discard items, remember the cost to the environment in producing and eventually disposing of them.

Reusing glass

In the UK, the returnable drinks market has almost been reduced to milk and beer bottling. Yet reuse and refilling schemes are still common in

---

Did You Know?

Sustainability over the long term depends on eliminating waste flows. One of the most obvious places to reduce the volume of waste generated is industry, where a restructuring of manufacturing processes can easily slash waste by a third or more. The 3M Company halved its hazardous waste flows within a decade of launching a corporation-wide programme. A pioneer in waste reduction, 3M also boosted its profits in the process.

Source: *State of the World 1990*, (Worldwatch Institute)

Europe, often as a result of legislation. Bottles for reuse are stronger and more expensive to manufacture than a one-trip container. But they will soon pay for themselves after several trips for refilling. Milk bottles can be reused up to 30 times – don't put them in a dustbin or in a bottle bank.

Water

Water is perhaps the most precious of all our resources, yet we treat it with disdain and increasingly threaten its quality with industrial and organic wastes.

An enormous volume of water is used in industrial and commercial activities and any processes should be analysed to find ways to reduce the amount of water used and to recycle it for another use. See Chapter 15.

RECYCLE

Recycling has of necessity captured the attention of people worldwide. Of course reclaiming and recycling materials is not a new idea; in some parts of the world people's lives depend upon it. But elsewhere many established schemes have highlighted the amount of waste created by western consumerist life. Recycling is one positive option for minimising the impact of waste on the environment. But it must always be remembered that recycling is third in the chain – after reducing and reusing.

One of the basic laws of nature is that nothing actually disappears when it is thrown away. As US environmentalist Barry Commoner said, 'In nature, no organic substance is synthesized unless there is provision for its degradation; recycling is enforced.' It is time we paid the same attention to the materials that we produce.

Many of the raw materials used for all sorts of products are finite resources – they don't last for ever. Using resources like oil to produce plastics for packaging is an energy-intensive process for a throwaway material. We need to make better use of limited resources and where possible use materials derived from sustainable or renewable sources.

Did You Know?

A small drip from a worn washer can waste 200 litres of water a day – and if it's a hot water tap you will be paying to heat the water.

In the UK established recycling schemes exist for scrap metal of all kinds (including aluminium), glass, paper, textiles, plastics and oil. Many other materials like wood are also recycled – the possibilities can be endless.

Some types of reclamation are still in their early stages; for example, CFC recovery and organic waste for composting. About 30% of domestic waste consists of organic matter – vegetable and food wastes as well as garden waste. Wastes such as straw and sewage are also suitable for composting. In all composting activities, attention needs to be given to possible heavy metal contamination in the original waste. But finding new disposal options for organic waste is very important.

Decaying organic matter in landfill sites produces a potentially polluting liquid (leachate) and methane, a major greenhouse gas. But composting stabilises this type of waste and produces a useful end-product – a soil conditioner or compost.

We need to take up the challenge of recycling more material. This demands co-operation and participation to ensure that maximum amounts of materials are reclaimed and that schemes are economic and sustainable. Partnerships between community groups, local authorities, the reclamation trade and waste disposal authorities can act as a powerful stimulus to recycling.

Case Study: Sheffield – 'Recycling City'

The 'Recycling City' venture was launched in May 1989 by Friends of the Earth and is based on a partnership between the local authority, government, industry and the voluntary sector with sponsorship from British Telecom. The idea is to create a 'best practice' scheme which eventually aims to tackle up to 50% of Sheffield's annual 250,000 tonnes of domestic waste.

The Blue Box scheme follows a Canadian example where householders separate their rubbish at source. Recyclable materials are put into separate compartments of the box which is collected on a door-to-door basis. The scheme is backed up by city-wide provision of bottle banks, paper and can banks, plastic collections and other recycling facilities for householders and workplaces not covered by the Blue Box scheme.

The effectiveness of the programme is being monitored with the support of the Department of Trade and Industry. Other Recycling City projects have now been established in Dundee and Cardiff, and Devon has set up a Recycling County project.

RECYCLING SPECIFIC GOODS

Aluminium cans

Aluminium cans are successfully recycled in the UK and new plants are being developed to increase the recycling rate. At present the UK is only recycling 10% of its all-aluminium cans. Retrieving more aluminium from the waste stream is crucial – recycling saves 95% of the energy it takes to convert bauxite ore into new aluminium.

Every effort should be made to collect all aluminium cans at the workplace. Aluminium cans that are not labelled as such can be identified using a magnet on the body of the can. (Don't use it on the top, as some steel cans have an aluminium end). Aluminium is not magnetic. All cans should be washed and squashed and placed in the collection sacks. Many of the can manufacturers will provide posters and publicity material to help you encourage more people to join in.

Glass

Glass bottles and jars can be recycled continuously without any deterioration in quality. Every tonne of waste glass (cullet) used in glassmaking saves the energy equivalent of 30 gallons of oil and 1.2 tonnes of primary raw material. Recycling also cuts the impact of quarrying raw materials – sand, limestone and soda ash. Support any bottle bank schemes near your workplace (or get one installed!). Remember that broken window glass, light bulbs and other glass products must not be put in bottle banks.

Paper

See Chapter 5.

Plastic

Plastic is made from raw materials such as oil, natural gas, and coal. Its long life makes it appropriate for durable and hard-wearing goods, but unfortunately too many of its uses are for short-life disposable products.

Development of recycling techniques has been hindered by the many different types of plastic: one product can incorporate several different plastics. Sophisticated technology using lasers can identify and sort plastics but widespread adoption will be hampered by cost.

Another problem is finding appropriate uses for reclaimed plastic which is often contaminated with other materials or other plastics. Recycled plastic has long been used as a filler for jackets and sleeping bags, but this is a low-grade use for such an energy-intensive material. Mixed plastic waste

> **Did You Know?**
> 10 billion foamed polystyrene cups are used every year in Europe. A pilot Save-a-Cup scheme was launched in London in 1990 with support from the Dow Chemical Company. One million cups are collected every month from special bins installed in 62 offices and factories in the London area. The cups are processed into non-food items.
> Source: *Packaging Week* (20.2.91)

is also used for making products like traffic cones and ramps where appearance comes second to durability.

Belgian technology has developed another use for mixed plastic waste – as an artificial timber which can be worked in the same way as wood yet is rot and splinter-proof.

The US industry has invested heavily in the development of recyclable and degradable products to prove that plastic can be recycled. Degradable plastics include those that are broken down by exposure to light as well as bacterially-derived plastics. The new market for degradable products has risen sharply in the US. By the end of 1989, over 90% of branded consumer rubbish bags were degradable, although many are not fully bio-degradable in the short term.

Within the packaging industry, the challenge is now on to reuse plastic as a packaging material suitable for food and drink. The day of the returnable plastic bottle has already arrived. Coca-Cola introduced a pilot refillable bottle scheme in Switzerland in 1990. The project proved so successful that it has been extended to other countries where returnable bottles still retain a significant market share. Any possible contamination of the bottles is picked up by ultraviolet light and a 'sniffer' device.

> **Did You Know?**
> The supermarket chain, J. Sainsbury, has initiated a 'new bags for old' scheme as a way of reducing the environmental impact of plastic carrier bags. Customers are given a rebate of 1p for every bag brought back and reused. Sainsbury's calculate that the scheme, which is being enthusiastically supported, will save 50 million carrier bags (1,000 tonnes of plastic) and the equivalent of more than 1 million gallons of oil a year.
> Source: *Packaging Week* (13.2.91).

AN EFFECTIVE RECYCLING SYSTEM

For recycling to be successful within a workplace an efficient system must be set up. Before you collect anything you need to check there is an end market for it – this is particularly true for the various types of paper.

An efficient system requires the following:

1 Appoint a recycling co-ordinator, and give them plenty of support.
2 A successful scheme depends upon information. Make sure staff are aware of the benefits of recycling certain materials. Posters and publicity material from the trade bodies (e.g. aluminium can manufacturers) will help encourage people to support the scheme.
3 Place appropriate bins, boxes or collection sacks at convenient locations throughout the workplace.
4 Ensure that you have a suitable space to store material until it can be collected. Be aware of any fire regulations.
5 Organise collection of the recyclable material by the reclamation trade, local council or private collectors.
6 Deliver material to relevant places for reuse or recycling. Refurbishment workshops will accept old furniture and some electrical equipment.
7 Any proceeds from the sale of materials could be used for improvements within the workplace or donated to local charities.

CLOSING THE LOOP

Recycling and reuse schemes are not just about collecting materials. To be economically viable, such schemes need there to be a strong market for goods made from reclaimed materials. Far more attention needs to be paid to supporting companies who are closing the recycling loop. Reclaimed materials can produce high quality products, but the emphasis should also be on using the most appropriate material for the right purposes. There is no need to use high quality office stationery for drafts or as scrap paper, when a lower grade paper will do the job perfectly well. All workplaces need to develop a positive purchasing policy to support these new markets.

CHAPTER 5

USING PAPER AS IF TREES MATTERED

'Wise consumption is a far more difficult art than wise production.'

JOHN RUSKIN

Forecasts of the paperless office have proved a myth. Just look around your own workplace and you will quickly realise how much paper is taken for granted. We often use it once and then throw it away. Over a third of the contents of a dustbin will be paper products and packaging.

Offices generate enormous quantities of high quality wastepaper, much of which is discarded and lost from the recycling system. It has been estimated that over 130,000 tonnes of office waste paper could be economically recovered and recycled every year in the UK alone. Think about that the next time you discard a pile of paper.

The paper and board industry is one of the nation's top consumers of energy. It therefore makes sense to reuse and recycle paper as much as possible. Recycling waste paper reduces industrial water use by 58%, energy use by 40%, air pollution by 74%, and water pollution by 35%.

Recycling waste paper means that fewer trees have to be cut down for virgin pulp and less paper ends up in landfill sites. With rising disposal costs it makes little sense to bury a potential useful resource.

The first action in using paper as if trees mattered is to change to using unbleached, recycled paper for all our uses. It makes economic and environmental sense and is therefore essential in any sustainable work strategy. 'Recyconomic' copy papers, produced by Zweckform, were one of the first of these and are widely available, although they are produced in

> **Did You Know?**
> The average person uses 130kg of paper each year – equivalent to about two trees.

Germany and imported from there. More, similar products are now coming on to the market.

One problem with going over to recycled paper has been photocopiers – or, more specifically, photocopy engineers attempting to blame failures on the use of recycled paper. Don't believe them! Ten years ago they might have been justified (recycled paper fibres are shorter and more likely to shed dust into the machine) but the quality has improved enormously. The use of Zweckform and some other papers has now been endorsed by certain copier manufacturers.

Recycled paper should be used for all an organisation's uses, not just for internal documents. Recent advances in paper technology mean that a variety of recycled papers are now available – from high-grade stationery and computer paper to the lower grade paper suitable for envelopes and note-books. The more we demand these products, the greater the response from manufacturers. This will bring benefits in terms of quality and price – as well as benefits to the environment. Adopting positive purchasing policies is one of the greatest contributions an office can make.

A bright white paper looks clean but producing it from brown wood-pulp is a dirty and polluting process. Chlorine bleaching produces dioxin, an extremely toxic substance capable of causing cancer and birth defects. Alternative bleaching processes are now available but think carefully whether it is really necessary to have all your office paper products – from toilet rolls to stationery – a brilliant white. In Germany the use of unbleached paper is used as a market advantage – to demonstrate the user's commitment to the environment.

OFFICE TECHNOLOGY AND PAPER

Technology should exist to help us in our work, to save our time and to assist us to take better care of our world. Instead it is often used thoughtlessly, wasting the time of many operators and harming the environment through its massive consumption of paper. Word processing is a prime example.

In any purge to cut back on paper use, consult the word processing operators first. They will be able to provide many examples of the

> **Did You Know?**
> In the US it has been calculated that enough computer paper is spewed out each day to encircle the world 40 times.

inefficient processes that occur. For example, reports being sent back for 'just a few changes', three or four times; letters to be retyped for a slight alteration; multiple copies of reports sent out continuously, and many more.

Photocopying and fax machines, although excellent in concept, also seem to be adding to the paper gobbling disease. Before you run off a photocopy or respond to a request to 'just fax it to me', ask yourself: 'Does this really need to be done?'

Sometimes a brief telephone call will do instead of a letter, especially if a reply is needed.

Investigate the use of electronic mail for your office. Here communication is done through the computer – messages and documents can be relayed to other users' screens without the need for printing everything out. Again time and money is saved and environmental impact is lessened.

SAVING PAPER

There are many simple measures that can be implemented to tackle the paper mountain. Enlisting everyone's co-operation will certainly make the task a lot easier. But this might be more difficult than it sounds. Ingrained attitudes against reusing paper, using envelopes twice and using scrap paper for notes rather than quality paper have to be broken down. It may help to monitor how much has been saved by adopting these measures. As an incentive this money could be used within the workplace or donated to charity.

Using the right grade for the right use is essential. Why use high-quality paper for rough drafts and internal memos? Some of the lower grades of recycled paper are more than suitable for this purpose. Make sure this message gets around the office.

Internal memo forms could be re-designed to save paper. For example, the sender writes the message (handwritten if short) on the left-hand side and the recipient replies on the right-hand side. Only if important would the recipient bother to keep a copy.

Here is an example:

MEMO	
TO: Mary Jones	TO: John
FROM: John Smith	FROM: Mary
DATE: 20/5	DATE: 20/5
SUBJECT:	SUBJECT:
Paper saving. Do we use recycled paper for all documents?	Yes, it is company policy.

Another version is to split the memo form horizontally, but the vertical split entices people to write in point form and the recipient can also easily answer point by point. You should also check the size of paper used for memos and letters. Could it be half the size?

Instead of writing or dictating a letter in reply to one received, simply handwrite the answer on the original letter and send it back. If you really need a copy of the letter, photocopy it before sending the original back to the sender. This efficient practice saves time, saves paper, saves filing space, the sender gets the reply quickly, and the organisation saves money by needing fewer typists and less stationery. If you dislike the idea of handwritten replies going out of the organisation, at least use this practice with internal company correspondence.

If the message to be sent with a document is clear and simple, don't send a memo, simply write the note on the front of the document itself. Or, if this is not a satisfactory solution, attach a small action slip with pre-printed actions ticked (as below). Make more use of small 'Post-It Notes' or small 'With Compliments' slips – they are both excellent paper and time savers.

ACTION SLIP:
　　To:
　　For approval please
　　For your attention/action
　　For your information
　　Please pass on to ....
　　Please return with comments
　　Please note and put in recycling bin.
　　Other ....
From:　　　　　　　　　　Date:

Issue instructions that only one draft of documents will be prepared and printed out – the next one is the final one. This action will focus the mind and ensure that originators of documents take more care with the alteration and correction of drafts.

Here is some more advice on saving and re-using paper:

Did You Know?
In 1989 the UK imported over two thirds of its paper and board requirements. This represented the second highest contribution to our trade deficit after automobiles. Recycling more waste paper could help save on our balance of payments.

- Reuse paper and envelopes wherever possible. Keep a tray in a handy position for reusable paper and envelopes. The backs of old letters or documents are ideal for scrap paper, internal notes or can be cut up and stapled together to form note-pads.
- There is no reason why envelopes, particularly the larger sizes, cannot be reused. Special reuse labels (gummed paper about 12cm × 8cm) with a conservation message are available from a range of organisations or a plain sticky label stuck over the old address will do the trick. If you decide to adopt this as a general policy you could think about producing envelope stickers with the company logo and a suitable message – another way of 'personalising' envelopes while publicising sustainable work practices.
- If you are reusing envelopes, you will have to take care in opening them. A paper knife will make a clean cut and the ends of large envelopes can be resealed with sellotape, a sticky label or staples.
- Reuse envelopes within the office. Envelopes are available with lines across the front and back so they can be reused by crossing off the name of the last recipient and re-addressing them.
- Encourage double-sided photocopying on recycled paper.
- Some methods of document presentation are very wasteful and should be discouraged. Do you really need to have double spacing on all drafts, manuscripts and reports? Why not reduce the amount of 'white space' around the borders of reports and in between paragraphs?

Some of these suggestions may appear unattractive at first. But when you consider the environmental impact of paper production and disposal, recycling makes sense.

MAILING LISTS

Computerised mailing lists can result in a tremendous waste of paper. Make frequent checks on lists to make sure that the names on them really need to be there. Selectively deleting names on mailing lists can be a good way of finding out if people really need the information or whether they just want to be seen to be on mailing lists.

With longer documents ask if everyone needs a copy. Could one copy with a slip, listing recipients' names, be sent round instead of multiple copies? This does require co-operation. Someone, at first, is bound to hold up the process which could lead to complaints. But persevere.

Take a fresh look at the mail you receive. In a large company it can be instructive to follow the mail delivery around and see how many copies of the same 'quasi-technical' journal are delivered in the building (and how many are thrown away unread!).

Ask section heads to ask all staff if they really need to get copies of magazines and journals that somebody else in the organisation already gets. Could a 'share and circulate' system be put into operation?

Junk mail is one of the largest contributors to the waste stream – it is rarely printed on recycled paper and is often discarded unread. Get your name taken off unwanted mailing lists by writing to the Mailing Preference Service (Freepost 20, London W1 7EZ). There is no charge for this and it will stop your name being added to more lists. To tackle the lists your name is already on, send back unwanted, unsolicited mail to the sender. Put a note on the envelope telling them to take your name off their list. Any rational company will be aware that it is not in their interest to waste money sending mail where it is clearly not wanted. Even the worst will, sooner or later, get the message that your workplace is not receptive to such practices.

GENERAL PAPER-SAVING PRACTICES

- Re-think all your workplace uses of disposable paper products. Eliminate the use of paper towels in the kitchens and toilets and get cloth roll towels supplied. These are much less polluting than either paper or hot-air driers.
- Get staff to take along their own cups to coffee machines rather than using disposable paper cups. You could also produce a range of company coffee mugs for general use (and support your local pottery in doing so!).
- Use unbleached, recycled toilet paper.
- Reuse paper bags again and again.
- Set up communal newspaper buying. Request that a few copies of the morning newspapers are bought and placed in strategic places throughout the building. People can read them throughout the day and old newspapers can then go to recycling collections. This system works in libraries and should work equally well at your workplace.

RECYCLING PAPER

This is one of the most basic aspects of 'working greener' and it's one that almost everyone will understand. More and more organisations are recognising the benefits of setting up recycling programmes, and more businesses are developing that will take away office paper. The Paper Recycling

Company, a new London-based business, recently signed up Jaeger and the Bank of Tokyo along with literally hundreds of other interested companies. But an office recycling scheme does need to be efficiently run, otherwise people will lose their initial enthusiasm. Such schemes are always harder to revive.

Steps to an effective paper recycling programme

- Appoint a recycling co-ordinator to be in overall charge of the recycling scheme. This person should be a member of your SWAG (or similar group). If necessary appoint co-ordinators for each floor of the building to ensure the smooth working of the scheme. It is also important to discuss the possibility of a collection scheme with your cleaning staff at as early a stage as possible: they will need to know how to incorporate the changes into their working and may also have useful suggestions on storage, etc.
- Before you start collecting any paper within the workplace, check out the markets for it. There may be a well-established office paper collection scheme operating in your area or you might want to sell direct to a waste paper merchant. If you choose the latter course of action you might want to donate the proceeds to charity.
- Having established the contacts and checked which type of paper is needed, you need to be aware that recycling will mean sorting. The type of paper most in demand is white office paper and computer paper. These grades are useful wood pulp substitutes and produce a high-quality paper. Very few merchants will take old newspapers.
- One way to collect is for everyone to have a recycling tray or box on or under their desk. When full this is emptied into a central collecting bin to await collection. Make sure you find out the minimum quantities needed before anyone will collect from you. You may need to find fire-proof storage space within your building.
- Good publicity is vital for the success of any scheme. Make sure you let people know what is going on and how they can help. Publicise the recycling scheme in any in-house newspaper or magazine. Make sure new staff are made aware of the scheme.
- As well as desk bins it is also a good idea to have collecting bins near photocopiers and computer printers – any discarded paper can then go straight in the bin.
- Make sure all the collection points have a notice on them explaining which type of paper is not suitable. Other materials such as laminated or varnished covers, sellotape, and papers bound together with

certain types of adhesives (as in the binding of a book) are contaminants and can substantially hinder any recycling process. The same is true of self-seal envelopes.
- Computer paper may be worth collecting separately if your workplace accumulates enough – check with your paper dealer.
- Monitor the scheme to make any necessary adjustments.
- If the amount of paper you collect is relatively small, why don't you combine with another small business to make the paper pick-ups worthwhile?

The following types of paper should all be recyclable. (Remember that some of these items will be worth more if they are separated out. If in doubt, ask.)

- all drawings on paper
- photocopy paper
- bond paper
- writing paper and notepaper
- envelopes
- binder dividers or index sheets
- index cards
- computer cards
- computer printout (without carbon)
- reports (stapled)
- writing pads (remove backing)
- manilla folders (light brown)

Please note that fax paper cannot be recycled.

A few staples are usually acceptable but try to remove them wherever possible.

New business initiatives

Much of the early work on office paper recycling was the result of work by small recycling companies such as 'PaperRound', set up in London with the

---

Did You Know?

In 1989 over 2.5 million tonnes of waste paper were recycled in the UK into new paper and board products. This processing of waste paper compares favourably with other EC countries but it should be stressed that most went into packaging materials rather than new paper products.

active support of Friends of the Earth in 1989. Now one of the largest users of waste paper, Fort Sterling paper, have launched a scheme whereby they will collect office waste paper from any medium or large organisation throughout the UK. Their scheme involves working with the Independent Waste Paper Processors Association, a body that represents paper merchants throughout the UK. They publish *Completing the Recycling Loop Scheme* and can be contacted c/o 1 Peall Road, Croydon CR10 3EX.

NEWSPAPER, MAGAZINE AND BOOK PUBLISHING

Some of the greatest consumers of paper are the newspaper and book publishing industries. One of the greatest challenges for these industries, especially the newspaper industry, is to establish technologies to reuse the vast amounts of paper they consume. For such a short-lived product as a newspaper, there is absolutely no reason why a greater percentage of recycled material cannot be used.

A survey undertaken by Friends of the Earth in 1990 revealed that the UK's national newspapers were using a relatively low percentage of recycled fibre. The highest was 39% and none of the papers surveyed could give an overall minimum average.

Newspapers could now be using up to 60% reclaimed fibre, and one plant is even making 100% reclaimed newsprint. New recycling plants are coming on stream in the UK so newspaper companies need to start using a higher percentage of recycled fibre.

Real commitment is needed by the newspaper industry. In New York this is already happening. Publishers have agreed to increase their consumption of recycled fibre from the 7% used in 1989 to 40% by the year 2000.

Most of the UK's reclaimed waste paper goes into packaging but newsprint and the disposable paper industry are growing consumers. The paper industry also predict that new technologies will allow more opportunities for reclaimed fibre to be used in the printing and writing grades of paper.

The technology is already well established for printing magazines, reports, books, posters and other promotional material on recycled paper. Much of the paper for these comes from pre-consumer waste – for example printers' offcuts – or from high-quality post-consumer waste such as white office paper.

If you work in printing or publishing you can:

- investigate the use of recycled paper for all publications and packaging materials. Many paper companies are willing to send samples for you and your printers to try.
- try to replace the use of foam and plastic as a packaging material. Try shredded paper or card. One novel solution from a Dutch computer firm is to use popcorn instead of foam: this has proved very popular with birds and squirrels!
- recycle unsold or left-over publications. Investigate the use of water-based adhesives for book binding which do not inhibit the recycling process.

Case Study: It's not that difficult!

Green Print, publishers of this book, were set up in early 1988. They were committed to using recycled paper from the start. Their first book entailed the printer buying in sheets of recycled paper specially for the task, but since then things have changed.

The printers can now obtain high-quality recycled paper on reels so that it can be used on the larger 'web offset' machines and there is no difference in price. Director Jon Carpenter is categorical: 'Any and every publisher could be using recycled paper for books and the cost will be about the same.'

Over to you . . .

CHAPTER 6
ENERGY FOR WORKING

'Fossil fuels are not made by men; they cannot be recycled. Once they are gone, they are gone forever.'

E.F. Schumacher, *Small is Beautiful*

Reducing energy consumption through efficiency techniques and conservation measures is vital for future environmental protection. The threat of global warming sets serious limits on just how long the industrialised nations can go on consuming resources at the current rate. A policy based on doing nothing will result in unacceptable risks. But companies should be aware that adopting energy efficiency programmes does not mean sacrificing economic growth – they are a means of moving towards sustainable development.

Energy experts agree that improved energy efficiency is the best way to conserve energy and reduce our consumption of fossil fuels. In the UK this could be achieved without significantly lowering standards of living. But at the same time we need to be looking seriously at the commercial development of suitable forms of renewable energy.

It is already possible to burn less coal more efficiently in our power stations but the technology needs to be widely adopted. In our homes and workplaces we have to think seriously about the amount of energy we use and whether some of this could be saved by using more efficient appliances, by fitting energy saving devices or by extending the use of insulation materials.

A global goal was set at the 1988 Toronto Conference on the Changing Atmosphere to reduce carbon dioxide emissions by 20% by the year 2005 (based on 1987 levels), with a longer term target of 50% cuts.

Did You Know?

The UK uses about £40 billion of energy a year – about 8.5% of GDP. The Department of Energy suggests that *'simple decisions, taken by many individual managers and others, can save 20% of the nation's fuel bill, say £8 billion a year.'*

THE GREENHOUSE EFFECT

The greenhouse effect is caused by gases that have the ability to trap some of the sun's heat as it is reflected back from the earth's surface. Once trapped, the heat is unable to escape back into space. The result is an accelerating warming of the earth's surface.

Greenhouse gases are emitted as a result of many human activities but it is the scale of the problem that is causing international concern. Industry makes a major contribution by burning carbon-based fossil fuels such as coal and oil. These are used for heating and to provide power for machinery and road vehicles.

The US Environmental Protection Agency has estimated that 60-65% of greenhouse gases are produced either directly or indirectly by energy use.

GREENHOUSE GASES

Carbon dioxide

The increase of this gas in the atmosphere is largely due to the burning of fossil fuels such as coal, natural gas and petroleum for industry and transport; deforestation and changing land uses; and burning of vegetation/biomass.

Trees and plants have a major role to play in the planetary recycling of carbon, nitrogen and oxygen but destruction of forests can disrupt this cycle – meaning that less carbon dioxide is removed from the atmosphere.

Methane

Methane is a by-product of the bacterial breakdown of organic matter in swamps, rice paddies, and waste dumps. It is also emitted by ruminants such as cows and sheep and by some insects. Leaking coal and gas fields are other sources of methane.

Did You Know?

An authoritative report from the Rocky Mountain Institute in the US has shown that energy efficiency measures are seven times more cost effective at reducing carbon dioxide emissions than nuclear power.

Nitrous oxides

These gases are emitted from fossil fuel burning, vehicle emissions and from nitrogen fertilisers.

CFCs (chlorofluorocarbons)

These ozone-depleting chemicals are used in fridges and air conditioning, solvents, production of plastic foams and halons in fire extinguishers. (See Chapter 9).

RESPONSES TO THE GREENHOUSE EFFECT

The two principal responses to global warming from energy suppliers and consumers must be:

- increased energy efficiency;
- energy substitution – towards natural gas and renewable sources of energy.

The UK Watt Committee on Energy noted in 1990 that for buildings:

- two-thirds of energy savings could be made by improving insulation;
- the remaining third would come from improvements in the efficiency of heating systems, electrical appliances and lighting.
- better space heating could save at least half the current amount of energy used for this purpose.

Electricity

The UK's largest source of carbon dioxide emissions is from electricity generation – 205 million tonnes are released each year. Yet we use it inappropriately (for example in low-grade energy uses such as heating and cooling) and inefficiently (by leaving machines running when not being used). Electricity should be used for high-grade energy such as lighting and for powering electronic and motorised appliances.

Did You Know?

Natural gas produces at least 40% less carbon dioxide than coal and 26% less than oil. Natural gas also contains virtually no sulphur, unlike coal or oil, and so when it burns it produces little sulphur dioxide, the main contributor to acid rain.

Source: *New Scientist* (7.10.89).

In 1986, about 60% of UK electricity was used for the following purposes: space and water heating (23%); domestic electrical appliances and pumps (18%); lighting of domestic, public, commercial and industrial buildings (16%); and space cooling and ventilation in public and commercial buildings (3%).

Water heating

Electricity is an inefficient way to heat water, so consider a change to gas. Water is often kept at temperatures far higher than necessary so check your thermostats. Make sure that all storage tanks and pipes are insulated and that circulating pumps are shut down when the building is not occupied.

MAKING A SUCCESS OF IT

The success of energy efficiency plans will only be achieved if the supply authorities are committed to conservation measures and users of energy, particularly industry, are willing to adopt energy management practices. In some countries this is already the case.

Like all technologies, increasing energy efficiency will mean that money will need to be spent but the result could be significant. Using the UK government's own figures from the Energy Efficiency Office, Friends of the Earth calculated in November 1989 that spending £3.8 billion on energy efficiency measures would save nearly 20% of current primary energy use, cut CO_2 emissions by 30% from current levels, and save consumers more than £12 billion per year in reduced fuel bills.

Case Study: How the Dutch are cutting energy consumption

In the Netherlands the Dutch energy sector is planning a 13% reduction in the country's energy use by the end of the century. £435 million a year is being invested in energy conservation measures which will affect all sectors from households to industry.

In the power supply sector about 40% of the total savings will come from investment in small and medium-sized co-generation power plant improvements and from wind power. In the domestic sector savings of 12% are expected to come from the use of high-efficiency lighting whilst heating and lighting improvements in industry and government sectors will save 12%. Longer term measures which could save up to 33% of the planned savings would come from the expansion of district heating and using the heat from waste incinerators for power production.

ENERGY MANAGEMENT

The benefits of energy management may not be visible as a new piece of technology, nevertheless they do make a significant contribution to an organisation's productivity and profitability.

ELECTRICITY LOAD MANAGEMENT

Electricity 'load' refers to the demand a customer places on the electricity supply system. When electricity is offered at cheaper rates at different times of the day, substantial savings can be made by 'electricity load management'. Any large user should have discussions with the local electricity company with a view to making savings in this way.

ENERGY EFFICIENCY RATINGS

Statistics from the Building Research Establishment show that the UK's major contributor to carbon dioxide emissions is energy use (electricity, gas and oil) in buildings. But as well as improving building design and adopting better heating and insulation techniques (see Chapter 7) far more attention needs to be paid to using energy-efficient appliances. Many environmental groups are campaigning for higher minimum standards of energy efficiency.

The energy efficiency of the average domestic appliance in the UK is well below that of the best mass-produced models available in Europe. Yet there is a potential 75% energy saving to be made, meaning lower fuel bills for the user as well as a reduced impact on the environment.

In the UK consumer choice is limited and a lack of product information and labelling hinders a greater move towards energy-efficient appliances. Yet in other countries energy rating labels are standard practice. In Australia there is a multiple star rating. The more stars on the label, the more efficient the appliance. In the US and Canada there is energy labelling and legislation to ensure that minimum standards of efficiency are set for appliances. If UK standards were based on the United States measures, 90% of the appliances in our shops would be outlawed as too energy-inefficient.

If you are buying new equipment for your workplace ensure that you check any existing labels or ask for information on the energy efficiency of the product. This not only helps you decide on the best product but also keeps up pressure on manufacturers to include this information in product literature.

If you manufacture equipment, make sure that you are aiming at the highest energy efficiency there is possible for your product.

EQUIPMENT MAINTENANCE AND SERVICE

Significant energy losses occur if equipment is not kept in good order. Most equipment such as computers, photocopiers, motors, ovens and compressors will dissipate energy as heat. The most efficient units will have the least heat losses, so it is cost-effective to buy high-quality equipment in the first place. Check the power or energy rating on accompanying labels or equipment nameplates. If in doubt, ask. But even the most efficient units will need regular maintenance, so set up a servicing contract with the supplier.

LEAST COST PLANNING

Many electricity supply companies in the US are required to adopt least cost planning policies: this means that equal consideration must be given to managing demand as well as supply. This can be done by promoting energy-efficient devices or a range of measures from free energy surveys for all customers, to rebates for the purchase of energy-efficient lights or motors. In the UK the public electricity suppliers have a duty to demonstrate their commitment to energy efficiency by using least cost planning.

CONTRACT ENERGY MANAGEMENT AGREEMENT

Here an outside company will provide the necessary technical skills and advice for their clients as well as finance for energy efficiency measures. The resulting energy savings repay the cost of the investment and outside companies' services. Such a scheme has worked well in the private sector and it is suggested that such schemes should be used for local authorities and health authorities.

ENERGY CONSERVATION, CONVERSION AND CO-GENERATION

Efficiency measures include improved building insulation, installation of high-efficiency boilers, waste heat recovery, and management of water temperatures and flow.

RECOVERY OF WASTE HEAT

Successful energy management will involve the recovery of heat which most industries regard as waste. One third of the energy output of a gas engine is converted to mechanical energy; the remainder is rejected as heat which can easily be converted for other purposes. Suitable applications include space heating, drying, washing, and for commercial and domestic hot water.

The payback period is the time in which the cost of implementation is recovered in energy savings. Many energy management investments are quickly cost-effective.

EFFICIENT BOILERS

Conventional modern boilers lose 30% of their heat up the flue, in the form of water vapour from the burning gas. Yet gas condensing boilers can recover much more of this waste heat and potential resource. They only lose about 11% of the heat and although they are more expensive to buy initially, they are cheaper to run and will pay for themselves within four years.

They are suitable for both homes and offices. In 1988 Harlow District Council invested £21,000 in gas condensing boilers and in one year saved £18,000 on heating bills.

Case Studies: Saving heat

Kwikseal Products – part of DRG (UK) Ltd – produce foam sealants and adhesives. Solvents produced during the drying process resulted in odour problems until a new plant was built in 1986. This included a thermal oxidiser which incinerates 95% of the gaseous solvents. At the same time enough heat is recovered to heat all Kwikseal's ovens. The payback period was under 3 years.

Kelloggs (UK) have installed a central energy monitoring system to optimise environmental conditions and to maximise energy consumption. Waste steam is recovered for use in heating water and electricity consumption is carefully controlled according to demand. In the US, an energy task force of supervisory and technical personnel are present in each manufacturing location.

HEAT PUMPS

A heat pump is a device which extracts energy from a low temperature source, upgrades or downgrades it, and transfers it to wherever it is required as heating or cooling.

Heat pumps can make use of solar or waste energy. For example, they can take in air from outside the building, upgrade it and transfer it into the building as space heating. Or they can utilise low grade waste energy from industrial processes, which is particularly useful when the temperature of the waste is too low for conventional waste heat recovery systems.

They are energy efficient and have the ability to transfer far more energy than they consume (for example, for each unit of energy supplied to drive the system, a heat pump can provide an output in excess of three units of energy).

The largest potential market for heat pumps is space heating, although they can also be used for process heating, drying and cooling. They can be driven by electricity or gas and need to be sized correctly by qualified people.

CO-GENERATION OF ELECTRICITY AND HEAT

Electricity generation in large power stations is only approximately 35% efficient and the rest of the heat is usually dispersed as waste through the large cooling towers. This is extremely wasteful and the lost heat could be captured to be reused within the industry as process heat. Much more attention needs to be paid to this form of energy conservation using waste heat from power stations or industrial processes.

In combined heat and power (CHP) plants the steam can be used to produce hot water. This can then supply neighbouring buildings with hot water and heating (as in district heating schemes). In energy conservation terms the savings can be as much as 50%. Many other countries have used district heating for years. It has been described as 'heat on tap' for the

---

Case Study: CHP for Manchester Airport

Most of the electrical and space heating needs of a new terminal at Manchester Airport is to be met by a combined heat and power plant designed by Mowlem Engineering. Engine-driven generators will produce 9.7 MW of electricity and their exhaust gases will generate 5.4 MW of heat. It is expected that the £5 million scheme will save an estimated £1.5 million a year and will supply more than 70% of the airport's power and heat requirements.

receiving buildings, which don't need boilers or pumps, just pipes to carry hot water.

Co-generation does require initial investment but suitable schemes will repay this over a short period.

Through co-generation schemes the efficiency with which energy is used can be raised from 35% to as high as 75% or more. Furthermore, the use of waste heat will in itself tend to reduce electricity demand, particularly when the electricity is used for heating purposes.

Many European cities – Copenhagen and Hamburg, for instance – have co-generation schemes. By improving energy use, co-generation leads to fuel saving, reduced energy costs and less pollution.

RENEWABLE ENERGY SOURCES

Renewable resources include solar, wind, wave and biomass (fuel from plant and animal material). Wind and wave energy sources have not been developed sufficiently for use in most workplaces yet, although the future for wind power looks promising.

The future for renewables in the UK has received a further boost from the electricity privatisation programme which makes provisions for a non-fossil fuel obligation – 20% of electricity generated needs to come from sources other than fossil fuels.

WIND POWER

Figures produced by the British Wind Energy Association demonstrate that Britain could generate 20% of its future power from wind turbines. These figures have been publicly supported by the Department of Energy and the former Central Electricity Generating Board.

In order to harness the wind for electricity generation on a significant scale, groups of wind turbines (wind farms) would be needed. Examples of these are already operating in California, Denmark and the Netherlands. There is already an increasing small-scale use of wind generators in rural locations – both for workplaces such as the Centre for Appropriate Technology in Wales and for domestic use.

SOLAR POWER

Research into solar and biomass uses has gathered momentum worldwide, and these should be considered for any potential uses at your workplace. In

> **Case Study:** Solar powered parking meters
>
> Shepparton (dubbed the Solar City) is the first city in Australia – and the second in the world – to introduce solar powered parking meters.

a climate such as Britain's the best potential for using solar energy comes from passive solar design – using a building's form and construction materials to capture and store the energy received. This can help reduce heating and lighting bills.

The UK Department of Energy see passive solar design and cost-effective energy measures becoming well established in Britain by the mid 1990s.

Active solar technology and photovoltaics are established systems of generating energy but have suffered from a lack of funding for research and development in the UK. Britain has a number of companies working in the photovoltaic industry – one of the biggest applications is consumer goods such as watches and calculators. They can also be used for goods such as billboard and road signs and even parking meters.

In many countries solar water heating is a well-developed technology and should be investigated when any workplace needs to replace its water heating.

Solar power technologies are not sufficiently advanced to supply base electricity loads but could be used to boost energy supplies during the period of peak daytime energy consumption. In places such as Australia where the sun is plentiful, solar powered technologies provide power for amenities blocks, domestic water heating, swimming pools and other such facilities.

BIOMASS

Biomass sources include forestry and crop wastes, municipal and industrial wastes, sewage and various energy crops. The potential for biomass use is extremely large even in countries like the UK. For example, the Department of the Environment has suggested that 25% of the material buried each year in municipal tips could be economically converted into useful energy.

Worldwide the burning of fuels from plant and animal sources provides energy for much of the world. But using the by-products to produce more useful products (such as landfill gas) can be a more energy-efficient way of utilising resources. (See Chapter 11).

CUTTING THE FUEL BILLS

Straightforward conservation measures can save money, often with little or no expenditure:

- Remember to switch off lights, heaters and equipment when not needed. Closing doors keeps the heat in too.
- Water heaters should be switched off at night unless off-peak electricity is being used.
- On a weekly basis, thermostat settings should be checked. Calculating energy use from regular meter readings can prove to be useful in longer-term energy planning.
- On an occasional basis, ensure that routine maintenance of heating systems is carried out with any necessary changes to thermostat settings or water temperature. Ensure that lighting is kept free of dust.

STEPS IN AN ENERGY MANAGEMENT PROGRAMME

For most businesses, the annual expenditure on all energy ranges from 1-10% of turnover. Energy efficiency measures that result in a money saving of up to 20% of the current energy bill will usually be an achievable target. Remember that every £1,000 saved in energy costs is an extra £1,000 pre-tax profits.

Here's how you might set up an energy management programme:

1 Get endorsement of an energy policy by top management and publicise this policy to all employees. You might aim:
   a to minimise the company's use of energy consistent with its operational demands;
   b to purchase this minimised energy requirement at least cost.

2 Delegate specific responsibility at senior level to ensure this policy is implemented and let all relevant staff know who your new 'energy king/queen' is and what he or she will be doing.

3 Investigate the past and present use of energy, seasonal changes and the production-related components of the total energy bill. Examine the areas of high energy consumption. This will often entail submetering electricity and/or other fuels to obtain the necessary data for determining future strategies. Monitoring and targeting (M&T) for energy use should be likened to (and linked to) financial budgeting.

4 Discuss with those concerned the best possible ways of reducing energy consumption. Remember to include the financial implications when choosing the most appropriate courses of action. You could also include short, medium and long-term goals. Some examples might be:
- improve the standard of thermal insulation or combustion equipment;
- check automatic control equipment and, if necessary, adjust the settings;
- carry out plant efficiency trials;
- alter processing schedules to see if greater output can be achieved with the same amount of energy, or if the same output can be gained with less energy;
- change from electricity to gas for space and water heating.

5 After implementation, you need to check that the estimated savings are being achieved.

6 Have the alterations had the desired effect or have they produced some unforeseen effects which need tackling?

7 Re-examine the results and accept suggestions for further improvements.

At all stages of an energy management plan there should be full communication between management and employees. The energy consequences of all decisions should be open for comment.

The services of an energy consultant may be needed by a company to maximise its potential for saving energy. Energy audits are now offered by an increasing number of companies. It is also possible to hire metering equipment that allows energy use to be monitored. The information gained from an audit will provide valuable data for your energy management programme and the cost of such services will usually be repaid many times by the energy savings identified.

CHAPTER 7

ENERGY-EFFICIENT BUILDINGS

'When you build a thing you cannot merely build that thing in isolation, but must also repair the world around it, and within it, so that the larger world at that one place becomes more coherent, and more whole; and the thing you make takes its place in the web of nature, as you make it.'
　　　　　　　C. ALEXANDER *et al, A Pattern Language,* (New York, 1977)

Sustainable work require buildings that are both aesthetically pleasing and energy efficient. Offices and public buildings are full of equipment, synthetic materials and chemicals that can have an effect on human health – 'sick building syndrome'. But with proper care the introduction of energy efficiency measures should not lead to any increase in this problem.

It is unlikely that you will be about to build a new office or factory, but the suggestions for energy-efficient buildings can be incorporated within most existing buildings in many imaginative ways. Just knowing what leads to better utilisation of energy can give the committed person some ideas for how to save on both heating and lighting bills, and consequently carbon dioxide emissions.

Buildings use around half the energy consumed in the UK yet efficient building design can have a dramatic impact on the energy needed for heating, cooling and lighting. Many other countries are way ahead of the

> **Did You Know?**
>
> In 1987, the generation of energy consumed in buildings produced almost 300 million tonnes of carbon dioxide – more than twice the level produced by either industry or vehicles.
>
> 　The UK's revised Building Regulations (1990) now set standards for energy conservation that are equivalent to those in force in Sweden 50 years ago.

UK in making productive use of passive solar energy. But examples such as Milton Keynes Energy Park are demonstrating that such techniques are possible without massive extra building costs. The need for less air conditioning and lighting means that it need cost no more to build an energy-efficient building than an inefficient one.

DESIGN

Energy-efficient design takes into account:

Orientation and the potential to maximise solar gain

The south side of any building will be the warmest all year so simply siting buildings with large glazed areas facing south will result in solar gain. Passive solar design uses a building's form and material to capture, store and distribute solar energy. Integrating passive solar with other energy efficiency measures such as adequate insulation and controls on heating systems can make substantial energy savings in commercial buildings.

The Department of Energy estimate that a saving of at least £230 million by the year 2025 could be achieved by adopting passive solar technology.

Heat storage

Building materials such as concrete and brick are good thermal building materials.

Insulation

This can include draughtproofing, cavity wall insulation, roof and ceiling insulation and double glazing. The use of materials such as fitted carpets can help prevent heat loss through floors. Aluminium foil installed behind radiators can help reflect heat back into the room. Up to 25% of heat from a radiator fixed to an outside wall can escape if it is not shielded in this way.

Industrial and commercial premises often have only single skin walls and a large area that needs to be heated. Up to 35% of a building's heat can be lost through the walls so insulation can help cut fuel bills.

Ideally, external walls should be insulated during construction but it is possible to add insulating cladding to the exterior of a building at a later stage. One main advantage of this form of insulation is that it increases the thermal capacity of a building so that the drastic variation in temperature, which happens when a wall is uninsulated, does not occur. Instead the walls warm up and heat is re-radiated into the interior. Interior linings do not have this effect. In summer the exterior insulation protects against heat gain and therefore the building remains cooler. In older properties exterior wall insulation can cut out condensation problems and can weatherproof walls.

Cavity wall insulation with foam or mineral wools is another way of keeping the heat in. There has been some concern about the use of urea formaldehyde foam – its use is already legally restricted in other countries because it is a known irritant and can release gases with known health effects. However there are other materials on the market which do the job equally well – mineral wool or expanded polystyrene beads. Cavity wall insulation pays for itself in 4 years and will go on saving your fuel bills indefinitely. Government figures reveal that cavity wall insulation has the potential to cut the UK's CO_2 emissions by 3.2 million tonnes a year and its fuel bills by £650 million.

Loft insulation is a must for any building since 20% of the heat can be lost if no insulation – or inadequate insulation – is present. The revised Building Regulations (1990) specify a minimum depth of 150mm of insulation material. The payback starts immediately.

All hot water tanks should have insulating jackets and again the payback is immediate.

Draughty buildings waste energy. Significant heat losses occur in many buildings, particularly shops, through doorways which are in constant use.

Case Study: Super-insulated houses of the future?

Well-insulated buildings are standard in Scandinavia but to prove that energy efficiency really does cut costs, several of Finland's super-insulated houses have been built in Milton Keynes. They cost £2000 more to build than a conventional house of the same size but the fuel bills are around £30 a year compared to £250 or more for a traditional house the same size.

Did You Know?

It has been estimated in the US that in fifty years from now, when passive energy improvements have been fully adopted in commercial buildings, this will have removed the need for 85 power plants, each costing over two billion dollars, and will eliminate fuel needs equivalent to twice the output of the Alaska oil pipeline.

Source: 'Energy-efficient buildings' in *Scientific American* (April 1988).

Encourage the use of devices such as door self-closers, double doors which form air locks, air curtains, plastic strips and other measures which minimise heat losses (and gains). Remember it is good practice to shut all doors, and fire doors should never be propped open.

Badly fitting windows can lose a lot of heat and, if possible, should be double-glazed. If this is out of the question, there are a range of DIY draughtproofing materials available. Even foam strips fitted around window frames and metal strips fixed to the bottom of doors can be effective in keeping the heat in.

When insulating do not make the building too airtight. Without some natural ventilation, there can be a build-up of gases from central heating units and other equipment and materials.

HEATING AND COOLING SYSTEMS

Two-thirds of primary energy is lost during generation and transmission of electricity. As electricity is such a high-grade form of energy, it should not be used for low-grade uses such as heating and cooling. If possible, building design should maximise gains from passive solar power and gas should be used for heating purposes. All heating devices should have thermostats installed as well as improved control systems. The use of heat pumps should also be investigated (see Chapter 6).

LIGHTING

Lighting is an important issue when we are looking at ways to cut energy consumption. In the commercial sector, lighting accounts for over one third of the electricity used in commercial buildings. Yet energy-saving

---

Case Study: Energy-efficient buildings

Milton Keynes, the UK's most energy-efficient city, has set strict standards for new buildings. It has developed its own Energy Conservation Index which has to be adhered to before planning permission is given. The result is that the city now has over 1,000 buildings with thicker insulation, highly efficient boilers and passive solar heating. The Milton Keynes Development Corporation states that the construction costs for houses to this standard are less than 1% higher than for conventional buildings yet the heating bills are 30-40% lower.

IBM has made energy efficiency company policy and sets percentage targets for curbing energy use. Over 15 years IBM has cut £3 million from its energy bill for lighting alone.

developments such as compact fluorescent light bulbs can make significant savings as well as cutting down CO_2 emissions.

During its lifetime an ordinary 100-watt bulb can use up to 75 times more electricity than a fluorescent tube or compact bulb. Most of the energy consumed is actually given off as heat rather than light. But substituting a compact fluorescent bulb for a traditional bulb will keep half a tonne of carbon dioxide out of the atmosphere over the lifetime of the bulb. The lifetime of these new bulbs is five times as long as for traditional bulbs and although they are more expensive to buy, the energy savings will make a significant reduction to your electricity bills.

Low voltage lighting which operates at 12 volts instead of 240 volts is expected to feature heavily in an energy-efficient future. Low voltage systems can use 50-watt light bulbs to produce the same output as a conventional 100-watt bulb, therefore saving on electricity. They are already in use in shops and offices – as spotlights or downlights. Seek advice on whether these systems would be applicable for your workplace.

Attention to building design can decrease a building's dependence on artificial light. The Building Research Establishment has estimated that the energy equivalent of around 1 million tonnes of coal a year could be saved by the year 2020 in commercial and industrial buildings through a combination of architectural measures: these would make more daylight available and improve lighting controls.

Making the most of the natural lighting you have is essential. Here are some points to consider:

- On a small scale, skylights offer the opportunity to bring light into the workplace with little cost.
- Wherever possible site workplaces near windows and install photo-cell switches to turn lights near windows on and off automatically.
- All light fittings and bulbs need to be cleaned regularly to maximise their output.
- Attention must be paid to choosing the right light for the job. For example, poorly fitted fluorescent lighting can make VDU work in an office difficult due to reflections. The installation of uplighters using

---

Case Study: Savings at Edinburgh University

Edinburgh Unversity halls of residence changed their **740** conventional light fittings (100-watt bulbs) to 16-watt 2D compact fluorescent lamps. In the first year, savings of £17,000 were made – paying for the new equipment in only 9 months and savings 283 tonnes of CO_2 from being produced.

high pressure sodium (SON) lamps can ease this problem as well as being 8 times more efficient than ordinary lightbulbs.

LOOKING TO THE FUTURE

New developments in window materials are under way. Pilkington Glass are developing new glazing materials, whilst researchers at the Advanced Environmental Research Group in Cambridge, Massachusetts have developed a holographic diffractive structure (HDS). This bends the light coming through the window and dircts it to another area. The application of this glazing to windows in offices would make it possible to delivery daylight to areas of the office usually untouched by natural light.

BUILDING DESIGN RATING SYSTEMS

In an era of increased awareness of the impact that a building can have on both the local and global environment, an environmental assessment rating has been launched by the well-respected Building Research Establishment (BRE). The voluntary rating, known as BREEAM (Building Research Establishment Environmental Assessment), has been developed for assessing offices at the design stage and will in future be extended to other types of building use. BREEAM looks at building design in relation to thermal information and materials, proposed heating and cooling systems and other equipment.

Case Study: £700 saved per shop

Next Retail Ltd have saved an average of £700 a year per shop by installing energy-efficient 2D lights for general purpose lighting with low voltage spotlights for display areas (and where high colour definition is needed).

Case Study: Light into heat

A German company has developed a transparent insulation material that can convert daylight into useful heat. Daylight passing through the material is converted into heat as it strikes a dark coating on the surface of the insulating material. This system has been used in a building at the University of Strathclyde, Scotland and has already provided 80% of heat requirements and a saving of £70,000 per year.

If you want to make some changes in your workplace, some of the points raised by BREEAM would make a useful starting point. Contact the Building Research Establishment, Garston, Watford WD2 1QQ.

OUTSIDE THE BUILDING

The outside of the building should be just as aesthetically pleasing as the inside. The use of trees and shrubs can act as a buffer against noise and the summer sun. Even a few plants and flowers can enliven a concrete area. Try to set aside a quiet area for staff to use in lunchbreaks or for small informal meetings. Quiet areas are often lacking in the workplace, and yet we know that quietness is an essential ingredient for creative thinking – and creative thinking is a resource we cannot do without.

Workplace car parks are often the most sterile of places. Strategic tree planting can green these areas as well as providing shade. Even a small hole dug into the tarmac will allow quite a large tree to grow.

In small areas like entrances, flat roofs and balconies flower or plant tubs can be placed to enhance the aesthetic appearance of your office. In large buildings the task of indoor landscaping is often handed over to outside specialists. The bills can be large and often exotic plants are used. Check first to see if there is anyone in your workplace who would like to take on the responsibility of selecting and looking after the plants.

By the incorporation of just a few of these suggestions into your workplace, staff and clients would be convinced, without any costly promotion, of your commitment to a sustainable world.

> **Did You Know?**
> *The average tree absorbs about 60kg of carbon dioxide a year while growing.*

CHAPTER 8
TRANSPORTING PEOPLE AND PRODUCTS

It is not only in the workplace itself that sustainable work practices need to apply. The impact of any organisation goes way beyond the doors of the factory or office. One problem that has to be faced by any organisation is transport. The facts are glaringly clear: motor vehicles are a major source of pollution.

If we are serious about tackling the greenhouse effect or acid rain we have to look to reduce the use of motor vehicles. That doesn't mean we have to abandon them; rather it means looking for the most appropriate form of transport for the journey that is to be made. Workplaces are a great place to start this for one very good reason: every day everyone who works in your organisation arrives at roughly the same place at roughly the same time. This leads to what is euphemistically known as high traffic density (traffic jams to you and me).

The key component of most traffic jams is hundreds of cars, each containing just one person. Reducing the number of one-person cars is the best place to start in cutting pollution (and in making the roads in our cities more usable at rush hour).

There are, broadly speaking, four ways in which people can get to work. Each one of them needs careful assessment if we are to develop a balanced and sustainable transport policy. They are: by car, on foot, by bicycle or on public transport.

Did You Know?

In the UK motor vehicles produce:
18% of carbon dioxide emissions
85% of carbon monoxide pollution
45% of nitric oxide pollution

CARS

CUTTING POLLUTION

In a recent survey over two thirds of the companies interviewed claimed it was policy to only use unleaded petrol in all company cars. A similar survey showed that less than a quarter had actually made the change! It is not surprising that some environmentalists are cynical about the commitment of business to going green.

Changing to unleaded petrol is the most basic and simple part of any environmental strategy. Lead in petrol is a proven brain poison, it is unnecessary and unleaded petrol is cheaper. The only explanations for not running your company cars on unleaded petrol are inertia and inefficiency. So your first move is to bring pressure to bear and get the change made. If you're not sure how or whether your cars can be converted your dealer will be able to advise you and organise the conversions.

The next step is the new cars. Any new car bought by your company should have a catalytic converter fitted. These devices cut up to 90% of the nitrogen oxide emissions that are one of the causes of acid rain. While retrofitting is usually impossible, there is no difficulty getting new cars with them as standard. Bear in mind that from 1993 *all* new cars sold in Britain will have to have 'cats'.

Think also about diesel cars. There are more of these on the market now and they are more fuel-efficient (and thus produce less carbon dioxide per mile). Bear in mind that they do need careful maintenance – a badly-tuned diesel can be a serious polluter.

The other way to reduce pollution from your cars is to think about the type of car your company uses. The 'macho' culture that has pervaded the company car market has led to some companies feeding their rising executives perks in the form of steadily larger cars.

Did You Know?

For every 100 passenger-kilometres travelled:
A car burns 9 litres of fuel
A jet aircraft burns 9 litres
A motorcycle burns 5 litres
A bus burns 1.4 litres
A high-speed train burns 0.9 litres
A cyclist burns none!

Given erosion of tax benefits for company cars in the 1991 Budget, this particular foolishness may be coming to an end: your company could take a lead by avoiding the top end of the market and choosing instead cars that do the job as cleanly and efficiently as possible. See the section below on 'Driving sustainably' for more ideas. Two environmentally-aware companies – The Body Shop and detergent manufacturer Ecover – only make one model available as a company car, the Volkswagen Golf 'Umwelt', generally reckoned to be the least polluting car available.

If your organisation does have any kind of car fleet it probably has a breakdown service agreement with the AA or the RAC. Both these organisations have lobbied relentlessly for more road building in what many see as a misuse of their membership fees. If you want a breakdown service that supports all forms of transport, take out a company membership of the Environmental Transport Association. Through arrangements with various vehicle recovery agencies they claim to offer a breakdown service as good as either of the large networks. They also operate a cycle recovery scheme! For more details of these services and of their insurance and legal services contact the Environmental Transport Association, 17 George Street, Croydon, Surrey CR0 1LA (tel: 081 666 0445).

CUTTING USE

Any organisation can take steps to cut down car use by its employees. Think first about how staff get to work. If you don't know, a quick survey will provide the answers. In urban areas there's probably a high proportion coming by public transport or by bike. Try and find out why those who drive do so and see what potential there is for reducing the numbers. Better encouragement for cyclists (see below) is one way.

Another is to examine the possibility of car sharing or car pools. Car pools work where there are several people coming from the same area who

---

Did You Know?

Car pools are still rare in Britain but in Los Angeles they are now much more common since lanes on major freeways, similar to bus lanes, have been set up which are prohibited to cars with only one person travelling in them! In Orange County, California a new 'car pool only' road is being built. New Californian legislation requires every firm employing more than 25 people to draw up plans showing how they will reduce the number of car journeys made to work.

arrive and leave at the same time and who have regular working habits. There are often problems but ways exist to solve them.

Car pools can be a boon to the company as well, given that there is often pressure for more car parking space. Think about how you might provide incentives or rewards for successful car pools.

If there are a sizeable number of people coming to your workplace from another area and there is no public transport (this is an increasingly common problem with out-of-town industrial estates and science parks) think about organising some. Lobby the local bus company to lay on some rush hour services (see below). Another alternative would be to lay on a mini-bus service from some central point (perhaps in conjunction with other nearby employers).

JOURNEYS MADE DURING WORK

Survey all those members of staff who travel as part of their work. This ranges from travelling sales reps to staff in the office who may have to work on two sites a few hundred yards apart.

For very local journeys encourage walking or provide staff cycles (see below). If staff are travelling to meetings ensure that cars are being shared.

Where there are staff who are doing a great deal of travelling think about encouraging them to plan for minimum petrol use. Circulate the ideas on lower fuel consumption below. You could also offer positive incentives to encourage a working culture where fuel economy is seen as being a desirable target. Get all staff recording their mileages and fuel consumption and offer rewards for the best miles per gallon recorded over a month (or the best sales made per miles travelled!).

Encourage motivated staff to work out their own 'carbon dioxide budget' – how much CO_2 they produce in a month – and look to see staged reductions through better driving and use of public transport or walking where appropriate.

DRIVING 'SUSTAINABLY'

There are a number of ways in which a good driver can achieve lower fuel consumption. Pass these ideas to all staff who drive as part of their work.

- Accelerate smoothly to a sensible cruising speed. Cruising at 70 mph can use up to 25% more fuel than driving at 55 mph. Driving *over* 70 mph is simply illegal and no company should encourage or condone it.
- Make sure tyres are inflated to the correct pressures.

- Don't rest your foot on the clutch or brake.
- Push in the choke as soon as the car will run smoothly without it.
- Don't carry unnecessary weight in the car.
- Decrease wind resistance where possible – never leave a roof rack on the car when it is not being used.
- Check mileage against fuel regularly to ensure you are getting best value from it.

WALKING AND CYCLING

Two methods of transport involve no burning of fossil fuel in their day-to-day use. If a journey takes ten minutes or less to walk, then that is probably the quickest way to do it, once parking the car has added time to the journey. If your organisation has separate departments near each other, encourage staff to walk between them (one way to do this is to encourage all senior management to lead by example and to walk as a matter of course).

The cycle remains perhaps the most efficient machine ever invented. It can help a person travel at twice their walking speed or more while using less energy. In some towns and cities cycling is a major form of transport – usually where major employers are based near the centre and there are few

---

Case Study: The Body Shop

The Body Shop employs some 600 staff at their main offices in Sussex. In 1990 they undertook a survey of transport used by staff. As a result of this they approached all staff and offered them a chance to buy a cycle through the company. Over 350 expressed interest and as a result the Body Shop entered into an arrangement with Raleigh Cycles to offer their staff one out of a choice of four models at 60% of the retail price.

This was backed by an awareness campaign about transport including a fact-sheet delivered to each employee. The company already runs a minibus shuttle to and from the local station and to local housing areas. A notice-board has been put aside for promotion of staff car sharing: employees can put up notices listing their travel routes and times and others can contact them directly.

Company car use is limited to those staff who need them and one model only is on offer. In late 1991 the company will move to a new site, adjacent to the local railway line but at some distance from a station: they have initiated a local campaign to open a new station on the line near the company base.

hills. In others cycling is rarer but everywhere it is increasing as a leisure activity.

Encouraging cycling should be a key part of a sustainable work policy. There are a few key actions that employers should take:

- Provide secure cycle parking facilities.
- Pay a cycle mileage allowance to encourage staff to use cycles for work-related journeys.
- Provide a changing area and shower at work.

This last could involve some investment but where this has been done organisations report a very positive response. It means that cyclists can wear appropriate clothing and can also work up a sweat on the way to work!

PUBLIC TRANSPORT

After walking and cycling, public transport is the most energy-efficient way of getting around. Despite this public transport in Britain is all too often inconvenient. Employers usually ignore this aspect of the lives of their staff but a concerned employer should look at the quality of public transport in the area of the workplace and lobby the relevant body if it is not adequate.

Questions to ask include:

- Do the local buses take your colleagues where they want to go without changing?
- Are the bus or train services very overcrowded?
- Is late-running a problem (leading to employees arriving late through no fault of their own)?
- If employees commute by two forms of transport (e.g. changing from train to bus) can they get a single ticket that will cover both?
- Are there satisfactory services to the workplace at times outside rush hours? Can staff get home if they work late?

Employees can be encouraged to make use of public transport by the provision of interest-free loans for season tickets for rail or bus journeys. In some companies employees pay such annual loans back on a regular basis, each week paying considerably less than they would have done for a weekly ticket.

TRANSPORTING PRODUCTS

A study of a heavy transport fleet indicated that better driving techniques could improve fuel consumption and cut pollution by up to 20%. It found that driver education and training programmes were a very effective way of improving technique and thus saving fuel and money.

Significant fuel savings can also be made by ensuring correct vehicle specifications: e.g. usage and load factors, engine size and type, gearbox and drive configuration, cab/body style, driver comfort and tyre type. Attention to all these details should be part of an audit by the transport fleet manager and part of a programme of sustainable work policy development.

Further fuel savings have been made by many companies simply by better planning of vehicle journeys and better location directions. These savings are immediately effective for little or no cost.

The nature of cargoes is a long-term environmental concern. Hazardous or explosive materials are regularly taken by truck through built-up areas. If a company is handling such materials it should ensure that:

- Drivers are well-trained and regularly re-trained.
- All company licensing for transport of such materials is in order and frequently reviewed.
- Drivers are given full information on the hazards of the materials that they are transporting, along with special protective equipment where necessary.
- Vehicles are well-maintained and equipped with hazard signs and the correct fire extinguishers.

Any review or audit of company transport policy should include a study of what material could be sent by rail rather than by road, thus making further savings on fuel and pollution.

Even organisations with no vehicles or products to transport will invariably use transport in all sorts of ways. Points to remember are:

- Information transport: London and other large cities support courier firms whose purpose is to get documents from one part of town to another in an hour or less. Using a fax can be a lot cheaper for some material but if a courier is essential make contact with and use a cycle courier firm. Cycles are usually every bit as fast as motorcycles and far less polluting.
- Firms with no transport of their own will occasionally have to hire vehicles. Go for the most appropriate vehicle for the task and ensure that, if petrol-fuelled, it operates on unleaded petrol. There are also

now ever more vans on the market equipped with catalytic converters – if your normal hire firm is unsure as to the state of their trucks, then it's time to check out other firms!

ONE STEP BEYOND

Sustainable working should not stop at the front door of the factory or office, but should be reflected in all aspects of your work. Bear in mind that your organisation has an impact on your immediate environment simply as a result of the journeys made to and from your base.

Such journeys can be a major problem for local people. If such a problem exists in your locality, your organisation shares the responsibility for resolving it. If business traffic is damaging the local environment, work with local planners to resolve the issue. Could vehicles arrive and depart using a different route that would cause less pollution or congestion? Would a series of traffic calming measures help minimise the problems? As a responsible employer and an important part of the community any organisation developing sustainable working policies should be able to take a lead in resolving such problems.

CHAPTER 9

RECOVERING, CONVERTING AND DISPOSING OF WASTE

'We have used the land, the air and the water as our garbage dump, and the dump is full.'

DAVID SUZUKI

Retrieving, reusing or reprocessing materials from industrial and post-consumer waste is an obvious way of saving energy and resources. It can also reduce air and water pollution. Yet in the past landfilling of waste has been a popular and comparatively cheap method of disposal. This has hindered the development of waste minimisation, clean technologies and recycling techniques.

But now, the 1990 Environmental Protection Act imposes a strict 'duty of care' on all waste producers and handlers. Current practices will have to be scrutinised and changes made. This could affect your workplace. Failure to comply could result in criminal or civil liability.

At the national level, the way forward to increasing the amount of materials we recover and reprocess is through an integrated approach to

---

Case Study: To care or not to care?

A survey in 1990 by the waste management business Effluents Services and reported by the *ENDS Bulletin* (See 'Further reading') revealed that many companies are unprepared for the new 'duty of care' requirements in the 1990 Act.

Only 60 out of 248 companies approached would take part in the survey. In these companies responsibility for waste disposal was held by a range of different posts, including a managing director, personnel manager, stock controller and a buyer. 36% of the manufacturing firms and 17% of the chemical firms did not know the disposal method for their wastes.

waste management. The policy of 'dispose, dilute and disperse' can no longer be tolerated. The result has been contaminated groundwater, marine pollution and a decline in air quality.

REDUCING WASTE

New systems need to be designed to enhance waste minimisation: their object will be to create efficient collection and recycling schemes and to ensure that any waste needing final disposal is consigned to well managed landfill sites. Incineration plants should operate energy recovery schemes.

Waste minimisation and recycling are important parts of an effective waste management strategy. The impact of tightening legislation and increased consumer awareness about environmental issues should not be underestimated.

If you manufacture products, it could pay you to take a closer look at the potential environmental impact of your activities. There may be very real opportunities for you to cut your own costs and energy bills by adopting a resource-conservation approach. Companies that don't make adjustments could find themselves losing ground in the market place.

Some questions to ask might include:

- What opportunities are there for reducing the amount of waste produced? Could processes be made more efficient so as to cut energy and resource use? Could waste materials be recycled within the production system?
- Are there alternative raw materials which result in less waste being created?
- How can waste be treated to ensure its safe and efficient disposal?
- How can products be designed for reuse or to aid recycling?

At the workplace, one of the first steps in waste reduction is to carry out an industrial waste audit. Audits will often highlight economic losses that have been occurring in the company and can result in cost-effective waste management plans being drawn up.

> **Did You Know?**
> *Dow Chemicals have a waste reduction programme under the banner of 'WRAP' - Waste Reduction Always Pays. As a result of this programme they have cut waste disposal costs at their plant in Kings Lynn by 70%.*

RECOVERING, CONVERTING AND DISPOSING OF WASTE

> **Did You Know?**
> The Department of Trade and Industry operates an Environment Unit to help businesses meet the environmental challenge. Information and advice is available on best practice in waste management and research as well as research programmes into clean technologies. (See Chapter 13).

Workplaces must constantly strive for best practice. For every piece of waste needing disposal, you need to ask: 'Is there a better way?' 'Could the waste be reused or recycled within the workplace?' (This is often possible with energy or water.) Or: 'Could the waste serve as the raw material for another process or product?' It is increasingly possible to 'swap' wastes with other companies through waste exchange programmes.

RECOVERING WASTE

Material becomes identified as waste when the original user has no further purpose for it and wants to get rid of it. Much waste is only material that is in the wrong place. Put it in the right place and it could turn into a valuable commodity.

Recovering waste can substantially reduce the amount of material ending up in our landfill sites and cut disposal costs. It can also create new commodities and open up business ventures. The following case studies show how some UK organisations are exploiting this opportunity.

CFC RECOVERY

International controls on chlorofluorocarbons (CFCs), halons and other ozone-damaging chemicals directly affect a wide range of businesses. These include manufacturers and users of refrigeration and air conditioning equipment, plastic foams, electronic and engineering components and aerosol and fire-extinguishing systems.

The phase-out programme initiated by the 1987 Montreal Protocol has been criticised for doing too little, too late. Subsequent international meetings have agreed to bring forward the phasing out programme and this is under constant review by the European Community.

The damage already done to the ozone layer cannot be rectified in the short term since CFCs are such long-lived substances. They are capable of remaining in the atmosphere for up to 100 years. But there is much that can be done within our workplaces to reduce any further impact:

> **Case Study:** Recycling CFCs
>
> West Germany was the first country in Europe to set up a national scheme for recovering redundant CFCs from domestic fridges and freezers. In the UK, progress has been slow but Iceland Frozen Foods has made pioneering advances. Its efforts to minimise environmental impact have led to increased sales of its products.
>
> As the company was already recycling gases in its commercial refrigeration equipment, it was able to adapt this technology for domestic use. Iceland began by recycling CFCs in redundant appliances and moved on to develop similar portable systems for engineers to use when carrying out repairs. Collected CFCs are bottled and then sent to ICI for recycling or destruction by high temperature incineration. Local authorities are now adopting CFC recovery schemes.

- If you are using CFCs and related compounds in products or processes, have you examined whether alternative substances could be substituted?
- If not, could you adopt better design and operating procedures to minimise emissions?
- Wherever possible, CFCs need to be recovered and recycled. If this is not possible, they need to be properly disposed of. Seek technical advice.
- All refrigeration and air conditioning systems need to be regularly serviced by professional people. The CFCs circulate in virtually closed systems so most emissions occur from component breakdown, from slow leaks caused by damage to seals or pipe connections and from escape during maintenance work.

Old equipment containing CFCs as a refrigerant needs to be sent to a CFC recovery scheme before scrapping.

WASTE DISPOSAL

Wastes needing eventual disposal can be buried, treated and released into sewers, incinerated or stored. For especially toxic and noxious industrial wastes like PCBs high temperature incineration is the only safe answer.

Several hundred million tonnes of hazardous waste are produced each year mostly in industrialised countries but increasingly in developing countries. Many disposal sites have not been properly regulated and now need to be cleaned up to prevent pollution.

Hazardous waste is a broad description for waste that 'presents an immediate or long-term threat to people or the environment'. Toxic waste is often used to describe a small group of substances that cause 'death or serious injury to human beings or animals' (World Resources Institute).

Most hazardous waste comes from industries that produce plastics, paints, adhesives, pesticides, herbicides, fertilisers, chemicals, detergents, synthetic rubber and fibres, and explosives. Chlorinated solvents and acids can be extremely hazardous if they leach from landfill disposal sites into local groundwater supplies.

All organisations who produce and handle hazardous wastes need to comply with prescribed collection and disposal methods within the workplace. They should also demand to know what happens to them after they have left their premises. Insist on higher standards if you are not satisfied.

WASTE WATER

Water is one of the commonest waste materials. Waste water from

---

Case Study: Waste not, want not

SECONDARY RESOURCES is a substantial venture involving a number of companies and a partnership with Birmingham City Council. Secondary Resources took over an old refuse-derived fuel plant from the council in 1989 and now handles waste on their behalf. Metals are extracted from the waste stream and the remaining material is converted to refuse-derived fuel and a low grade compost. In June 1990, Secondary Resources hoped that 92% of the waste could be converted into usable end products.

PRE-PRESS SERVICES LTD operates a graphic reproduction service. Film processing tanks use two principal chemicals - developer and fixer. The fixer was previously discharged into the drain without treatment. But now Pre-Press rents recycling units for the fixer which cuts the company's consumption from 15,000 litres a year to under 2,000 litres. The recycling units have extended the life of a batch of fixer from 36 hours to 21 days without any drop in quality and the units have allowed the company to recover a greater amount of silver. Significant financial savings have been made.

BLUE CIRCLE INDUSTRIES have tapped the enormous potential of using landfill gas for industrial use. Their Stone Gas Plant in Kent is now recognised as one of the largest and most advanced plants in the world. The company supplies gas to its own cement works as well as to a metal smelting company and an industrial minerals plant in the area. The saving on fossil fuels has been the equivalent to providing central heating and hot water to over 6,000 homes, for each year of operation.

industrial and commercial activities creates many problems because of the large volume of water, the often high pollutant content, and sometimes the increased temperature.

In workplaces where large quantities of water are used, or where toxic substances are used, it is imperative that all staff are aware of, and strictly follow, any regulations regarding waste water. Discharging toxic material into sewers is not only illegal but can seriously disrupt the biological treatment processes at sewage works. Discharging waste straight into water courses is illegal and can be equally devastating.

If you need to release waste water, prior consent must be obtained for any release of poisonous, noxious or polluting matter or any solid waste matter, including trade or sewage effluent, into controlled waters. These include streams, lakes, rivers and groundwater sources. Pollution control is essential since 70% of drinking water in England and Wales comes from rivers and streams.

The National Rivers Authority (NRA) controls consents for releasing potentially contaminated water into watercourses whilst the water service companies grant consents for discharges to sewers. If trade effluents contain certain listed substances such as heavy metals or pesticides, prior consent from Her Majesty's Inspectorate of Pollution (HMIP) is required.

In future, industry will be facing tougher controls on waste water releases. As well as the substances that have to be eliminated from the water supply (including pesticides and known carcinogens), less dangerous but still hazardous substances have to be reduced. The UK government is required to draw up a reduction programme for substances like zinc, copper, chromium, arsenic, ammonia and lead.

- Aim for best practice now within your workplace. Ensure that any spillages are treated and not washed into the drainage system. Full records of all such incidents should be kept.
- Waste treatment should ideally be carried out at the site itself or arranged through external waste management authorities.
- Even if your organisation does not produce waste water as a result of production, there may still be problems with water contamination (e.g. from oil spills in garages). Ensure that commitment to best practice and a non-polluting and conserving attitude towards water develops throughout the organisation.

INTO THE FUTURE

Many industries have previously been reluctant to invest large sums of money in waste treatment. But public opinion has changed and the general community is no longer willing to tolerate unnecessary pollution and health hazards caused by careless disposal of industrial wastes.

New attitudes are needed. Minimising waste, recycling and composting organic waste material should not just be seen as part of the solution to the solid waste disposal problem. They need to be reviewed as a means to conserving and replacing natural resources used in production processes.

Those industries committed to sustainable work practices will be those who move quickly to invest in technology to minimise the impact of waste and particularly hazardous substances.

CHAPTER 10

DEVELOPING GREEN PRODUCTS, PROCESSES AND SERVICES

'The voter, the consumer, the public at large are increasingly demanding higher environmental standards. Governments are using, and will increasingly use, their regulatory powers to insist on and impose such standards.'
MICHAEL HESELTINE, UK Secretary of State for the Environment, May 1991

The first aim of sustainable work is to create goods or services that are both economically and ecologically enhancing.

For our economic well-being we need to add value to natural resources and develop products and services that are saleable, exportable or replace previously imported products. For our environmental well-being these products should also be durable and cause minimum harm to the environment in their use, their manufacture and their ultimate disposal.

That is certainly a tall order. But if the challenge is great, so are the opportunities. The rise of 'green consumerism' and the increasing scrutiny of large companies by their consumers has led to many manufacturers becoming more forward-looking. While some 'green' products have been criticised as marketing ploys there is no doubt that a new type of consumer is emerging.

Concerned or critical consumers want to buy products that do not harm our natural resources, are long-lasting and use minimal packaging. They want to put their money where they think it will assist the environmental cause. But such products are as yet few and far between. It is here that the challenge lies for those who research, develop, design and manufacture our products, their packaging and our services.

It is essential that the providers of services or products approach this challenge in an honest and open manner, which includes a commitment to improve their own ways of working. Companies who fail to meet this challenge may suffer when looking to market so-called green products. While some are certainly cons (perhaps the worst example was the dyeing of paper products to make them resemble unbleached recycled paper!) others are less obvious but may nevertheless leave a company vulnerable to criticism, especially if the plants that produce the 'green' product are still polluting the local environment.

The consumer will need help in discerning the difference between a genuine green product and another that masquerades as one. This need has led to the establishment of 'eco-labelling' schemes such as the 'Blue Angel' scheme in Germany or the 'Environmental Choice' programme in Canada. The EC is now working to bring in a Europe-wide labelling scheme and detailed proposals for that should be announced before the end of 1991.

An essential part of such schemes is the 'cradle to grave' approach: the award jury do not look at just the product itself but also at its components and how they are made and at the wastes produced during manufacture, use and final disposal. Similarly the packaging of any product must be of a standard to at least match the product. Any new product being planned for the market now should be considered against the eco-labelling criteria for such products (if they exist yet) and a company should look to have all its key products receiving the awards.

But green consumerism certainly has its limitations of which any company developing a sustainable work programme should be aware. Any company thinking about developing a new product should ask not just the first two questions below, but also the third:

- Will manufacture or use of this product be harmful to people and/or the environment?
- Is this the best design; is the product durable, easily repairable and recyclable?
- Is there a *real* need for this product?

Those who have made a true commitment to caring for the environment will consider these questions carefully. They will also take into account the following factors before they choose one material over another to use in manufacturing or packaging:

- The amount and scarcity of feedstock materials, and the energy required for raw material extraction, processing and product manufacture.
- The type and volume of by-products that will have to be disposed of in hazardous or non-hazardous waste facilities.

- The products' recyclability and the extent to which the use of recycled materials in manufacture can reduce some of the environmental impacts looked at above.

SUSTAINABLE PRODUCTS AND SERVICES

Developing public awareness and concern are generating new opportunities. Some of these are in areas that are clearly linked to green concerns. The European Commission estimates that up to 1.5 million people in Europe have jobs in the environmental field, notably in pollution control or environmental management, and suggest that this figure could double by the year 2000. In June 1991, a consultancy report suggested that the expenditure on capital equipment and services needed to tackle twelve key environmental problems would be £140 billion over the next nine years.

There are clearly whole new areas of work developing: a report by the TUC listed five main areas for new 'employment opportunities in environmental protection':

- Pollution control – this includes waste management and recycling.
- Polluting industries – the need to clean up in these industries will create new jobs.
- Environment infrastructure – clean-up programmes and urban renewal create jobs (although many are short-term). Increased interest in the environment leads to more parks, forests, nature reserves etc.
- Environmental agencies and services – there will be a need for more people to administer the new systems.
- Environmentally benign goods – there are likely to be a range of new jobs in this area.

Waste management and recycling are among the most obvious areas for future development. The recycling industry has come a long way from the Steptoe and Son image of rag and bone men but it remains, in many ways, a low-tech industry. New techniques to improve waste recovery rates or to

Did You Know?
A recent survey by the ECOTEC consultancy concluded that the environmental management market in the UK is worth about £4.1 billion annually and that this figure is set to grow by up to 8.5% p.a. in real terms.

> **Case Study:** Trading standards
>
> Littlewoods Stores have produced a corporate Code of Practice on procurement of merchandise. It states that all merchandise produced for sale (in developing nations and elsewhere) must be produced in conformity with Article 55 of the United Nations Charter (which covers human rights aspects of international economic and social co-operation) and with local legislation covering workers' rights, minimum wages etc.
>   All their suppliers of textiles, garments etc. are expected to abide by this. When a buyer for the company finds that a supplier is failing to satisfy the code they 'are required immediately to cease trading with that supplier and/or report the circumstances to a higher authority within Littlewoods'.

recycle wastes previously considered unsalvageable are needed and represent a substantial opportunity. Every company that spends money on cutting waste and pollution is providing income for those who can help solve their problems.

Linked to waste recycling is waste minimisation and this includes saving energy as well as materials. This will have a major impact on design and the potential for creating business in low-impact and low-energy products and packaging is enormous – almost everything we buy is designed by someone!

Growth areas in Britain at the moment include services of all types, and already new businesses are coming into being with their green ethics as a major selling point. An important aspect of this has been fair trade with developing nations. The Body Shop has led the way by paying 'western' rates for supplies purchased in poorer countries.

The idea of fair trading is being developed by a consortium of organisations which include *New Consumer* magazine (see 'Further reading'), the World Development Movement and Traidcraft (one of the largest importers of handicrafts produced in poorer countries). They are about to launch a 'fair trade mark' for imported products which will be awarded where it can be shown that the goods have been produced and imported without exploitation of the local workforce. Any company that wishes to develop its work in this field would be advised to contact *New Consumer* for more information.

> **Case Study:** It's in the bag
>
> The 'Whole Foods' chain in the USA offer 5 cents off your bill if you bring you own carrier bag.

GREEN PRODUCTS, PROCESSES AND SERVICES

The development of sustainable work practices offers opportunities. Many new products and new ways of doing things have to emerge if we are to move to a conserver-based economy. But we must not be lured into thinking that the inherent problems can be solved by technology. There is a need for simpler ways of doing things rather than for more complex technological fixes.

Some of these simpler ways of doing things may well have been recently abandoned in favour of more 'modern' approaches that can now be seen as short-sighted and wasteful. Much of the effort to develop biodegradable plastic has come from public concern over plastic litter, often composed largely of discarded carrier bags. Lightweight and fully reusable canvas shopping bags are hardly a new invention but those companies marketing them are reporting increasing sales as the public start to reject their plastic equivalent.

Prior to the agrochemical revolution, all Britain's food was organically grown. By the early 1980s organic food had become almost unobtainable and was seen as a fringe issue. Now there is a steady growth of farmers

---

Case Study: The Ecological Trading Company

The Ecological Trading Company is an example of a company that has come into existence to answer a need that has arisen as a result of developing environmental concern. In 1985 Friends of the Earth launched a major campaign to protect tropical rainforests: it developed rapidly. A central part of the campaign focused attention on the way in which the indiscriminate felling of hardwood trees for the timber industry was accelerating rainforest destruction.

Timber users were asked to avoid tropical hardwoods unless they clearly came from sustainably managed forests, and it soon became clear that very few, if any, large-scale timber operations were working sustainably. While European hardwoods provide substitutes for many uses there was still demand for tropical woods.

After extensive research the Ecological Trading Company was founded and in its first two years has been able to build up working relationships with small-scale, minimum-impact forestry schemes in Peru, Ecuador, the Solomon Islands and Papua New Guinea. Timber is imported in 20-foot containers and the emphasis is on high-grade timber for furniture and craft uses.

The timber is marketed in the UK by Milland Fine Timber Ltd, Iping Road, Milland, Hants, GU30 7NA. Milland Timber also now produce their own timber polish using beeswax from a co-operative in Zambia with over 4,000 beekeepers whose hives are spread throughout the forest in the region.

looking to get off the treadmill of ever more artificial pesticides and fertilisers. Organic food is being seen as a high-quality premium product and those supermarkets that have invested resources in developing their organic ranges have seen consistent growth in sales.

RESEARCH AND DEVELOPMENT

While there is no shortage of ideas for new products Britain has been very short of investment in new technology and new ideas over the last decade. While we have seen the development of science parks and increased co-operation between business and the high-tech end of academic research there has been a depressing history of failure to capitalise on innovative ideas. There is evidence that we may also be losing out by failing to address problem areas of pollution control where foreign business is ahead and may move in to the UK.

The increasing interest in environmental issues may provide a stimulus to new development in some key areas. The way in which advanced technology is now starting to be applied to recycling – an industry whose image has normally been closer to rag and bone men than to computerised sorting systems – is an indicator of the way things may move.

Any company that is developing new products will be aware of the lengthy processes involved. However, given an increasing market, the development of greener products and services remains a major business opportunity. The following are some suggested steps from research to commercial feasibility for greener products:

1 Research
2 Concept
3 Patent application
4 International market analysis
5 Economic and environmental analysis
6 Focused research and development
7 Research prototype
8 Update patent and submissions
9 Review market needs
10 Application study
11 Design consolidation and specification
12 International standard specification
13 Design and development
14 Product engineering – 1st phase
15 Pre-manufacture trial

16 Pre-market strategy
17 1st phase manufacture
18 Trials and international application submission
19 Presentation of international papers
20 Full marketing and manufacture
21 Research and development: next generation
22 Economic assessment/adjust pricing strategy
23 Ongoing 2nd phase development of cost-effective product

It hardly needs to be said that the environmental assessment and review that must start at an early phase should proceed in parallel with all later work. Many products that have proved to be environmental problem areas – notably CFCs – were initially seen as positive solutions to earlier problems.

GETTING HELP

There is a range of agencies that can assist new businesses and these vary around the country. Nationally there is one principal agency for developing environmental products – ETIS, the Environmental Technology Innovation Scheme. This has been set up as a result of co-operation between the Department of Trade and Industry (DTI) and the Department of the Environment. The aims are 'to encourage innovation, improve environmental standards and help users or suppliers of environmental technology to become more competitive'. Their main areas of concern are cleaner technologies, recycling, waste treatment and environmental monitoring.

ETIS can provide support and also aims to act as a focus for collaboration between different organisations: typically this would be between a company and a higher education establishment or a government research institute. ETIS can be contacted via the DTI Environment Unit at 151 Buckingham Palace Road, London SW1W 9SS.

The DTI also run DEMOS, their environmental management options scheme, which looks to provide 'support for environmental best practice and technology transfer'. More basic help can be obtained through the DTI's 'Environmental Helpline' – tel. 0800 585794/fax 0438 360858. This is run in co-operation with the Warren Spring Laboratory, a major government research facility. The helpline is not restricted to business and is also taking queries from schools, local authorities and other bodies. They offer up to four hours of free advice – if a detailed inquiry needs more work they offer paid consultancy.

Another 'new opportunity for developing environmental technology' is offered by Euroenviron, an umbrella project involving companies and research organisations in 13 European countries. This is linked to the 'Eureka' initiative and more about both can be obtained from the DTI Eureka office at the above address.

The DTI have also produced a range of factsheets on certain environmental issues and a more detailed book entitled *Cutting your losses – a business guide to waste minimisation*.

There is also a range of environmental consultancy groups, varying widely in size and mode of operation. For more details see Part C.

PROMOTING YOUR ACHIEVEMENTS

If you are going along the line of developing green products and services it is obviously important to promote everything worthwhile that you do so that others will learn from your efforts.

Conservationist David Bellamy highlighted this at a conference on 'The Green Consumer Revolution' in December 1989 when he said: 'The market is now and will continue to be conservation-led. Put your own house in order. Lead, don't be led.'

He gave the following suggestions:

- Set attainable targets and beat your own goals.
- Don't have accidents but if you do, call in the media as well as the clean-up experts.
- Publicise your achievements internally: circulate material pointing out that 'last month our recycling scheme saved X trees – this equals Y acres in habitat.'
- Your vehicle fleet should be lead-free, using catalytic converters and should advertise the facts on the back.
- Install energy-saving devices and make them part of your corporate image: 'The energy-saving equipment in this store saved X litres of fuel today'.

While being aware of your achievements, be aware also of your shortcomings and of problems still to be rectified. It is essential that you avoid making any claims that cannot be justified and that 'green PR' is absolutely honest. Those companies that have promoted one green initiative as being a sign that they are a green company have laid themselves wide open to criticism. Any annual environmental report that highlights work still to be done is far more likely to be taken seriously than one that glosses over such problems. As demands for disclosure of information become louder and more persistent, so secrecy becomes more obvious.

It is important to promote our achievements to your staff, to the public and to other organisations in your field. An environmental policy co-ordinator (or someone from the SWAG) should be trained and able to attend seminars and conferences to outline the work that has been done. Make sure all your staff are informed by holding regular seminars open to all. These can outline progress and make people feel part of the change process. They will help to bring about a view that 'sustainable work works' and will enable staff to take pride in the initiatives and to discuss them with others outside the workplace.

Positive outreach to your local community is also an important part of this and some examples of how this can be done are given in Chapter 11.

PART C

MOVING FORWARD

It should be clear from this book that 'working greener' isn't something that starts and then stops. It's a progressive process that can move one step at a time. This book has covered the first steps but there are plenty more beyond and they lead in many directions.
Part C looks at four areas:

- Environmental audits and reviews - what they are and how they may be useful (Chapter 11).
- Developing a strategy document to show how you plan to develop your environmental policy in the long term (Chapter 12).
- Finding out what further information and services are available to companies wishing to develop sustainable practices (Chapter 13).
- Ways in which organisations are going 'one step beyond' and taking innovative actions (Chapter 14).

Lastly, Chapter 15 gives a complete summary of 'Actions for every workplace'. The appendices include a bibliography fur further reading.

'When one person tugs at a single thing in nature, he finds it attached to the rest of the world.'

JOHN MUIR, Founder of the Sierra Club, USA.

CHAPTER 11
AUDITS, REVIEWS AND ASSESSMENTS

Following the upsurge of interest in environmental issues in the late 1980s, a number of large companies announced that they were undertaking environmental audits of what they did and produced. These have usually been carried out by external consultants and the standard and quality has varied enormously.

Certainly it is vitally important to know what impacts the organisation has on the environment and how those impacts can be minimised. The question that must first be asked is: 'What is the most effective way to find out what we need to know?' A full-scale environmental audit is very rarely an appropriate first step.

REVIEWING YOUR WORK

A key part of setting up your Sustainable Work Action Group was the walk-through review. This is the best place to start for any company or any section, assuming the work is done by a person or persons aware of that section's role in the overall organisation.

The essence of such a review is that it provides two basic types of information. Firstly there is the overview: this helps show what the section does, what it produces, the nature of the main inputs into that production, the levels of energy use and so on. These will need to be considered in more detail later. The second aspect is the 'environmental housekeeping list': any review of this nature should come up with a list of points where action can be taken by staff with minimal expenditure over the next few weeks and months.

Examples of these might be:

- Draughty window-frames or double glazing in need of maintenance.
- Large amounts of white office paper being thrown away.
- Dripping taps in staff washrooms.
- Needless use of disposable cups.

Taking action on these will not save the world, nor will they make your company a model of green good practice! Taking action on these issues *will* show your staff that sustainable work practices affect their workplace, that such changes can in fact make it more comfortable and that sustainable working is not just about the 'big issues'. In addition action plans to deal with these issues can show positive results within a short space of time and make everyone aware that things are actually moving.

FIRST THINGS FIRST

To get the most out of this phase it will be necessary to have the active involvement of senior staff in each section. If those staff are to contribute effectively it will be necessary for them to understand the background to sustainable working. The best way to provide that understanding is through a training course. There are a number of bodies that can provide such courses, which might include units on:

- Basic environmental concepts: ecology, energy flows, and pollution.
- Critical issues: the greenhouse effect, air pollution and global ecosystem damage.
- Responses to the crisis: new legislation from the government and the EC.
- How this affects us: the broad environmental impact of the organisation and what it does.
- New ways forward: monitoring and auditing; the three Rs - reduce, reuse and recycle; Integrated Pollution Control; the Precautionary Principle.
- Sustainable working: what we're going to do; how we're going to do it; how we're going to benefit from it.

A one or two day course covering these issues will make staff far more confident about working with these new concepts. They will then be able to do their walk-through review in greater detail and produce a more detailed plan of action.

TAKING IT FURTHER

Sectional reviews are, by definition, limited. Many sections have no control over the inputs they use or what happens to their outputs. There is also no consideration at this level about how the sections interlink and overlap.

The SWAG should therefore look to bring all section leaders together soon after they have undertaken their reviews to produce a company-wide action plan. Some of the points they raise will be common to many (e.g. basic energy-saving measures) and action can be initiated immediately. Others will be specific and may need detailed analysis.

The key to this stage is consideration of what they could not look at in their reviews - the ways in which they interact. The SWAG and its co-ordinator will have an important role in helping the staff identify these areas and sort them into ones where some action can be taken or where more detailed research is needed.

While in the first instance the review should be carried out by staff within their own section, there is no reason why follow-up reviews should not be done by staff from other sections reviewing each other's work. These 'exchange audits', which are already used by companies including British Steel, should not be seen as competitive but as an opportunity to let a fresh eye look at an area of work. They should in this way produce new ideas for positive action.

Out of all this comes the first stage in the organisation's plan (see Chapter 12). There will be changes in every section and these should be phased in carefully. This process has also hopefully produced a set of targets for further research and long-term action. Some of the questions that might be asked here are:

- What is the full environmental impact of the waste from our plant and how can it be minimised?
- How long will it take for major expenditure on energy efficiency to pay for itself?
- What control do we have over the source materials that we use and what policies exist to ensure that we attempt to purchase those with minimal environmental impact?

Some of these questions may need detailed research to answer them. It may be possible to carry this out in-house, or it may be that this is the point at which to bring in an environmental consultancy. This could be the beginning of what is often seen as an 'environmental audit'. It should be clear that, as a result of the first process, you will be in a far better position to brief the consultants on exactly what you want. This will save a great deal of time and money and should mean that you get a better report.

DETAILED SELF-ASSESSMENT

There are now a number of self-assessment guides on the market. These will look at the topics outlined above but will also take your organisation further down the audit path without having to commit it to hiring specialists. As with a review, these are not a substitute for a detailed audit but are a valuable step forward nonetheless. The Business in the Environment work-book should be the most up-to-date but others are also worth examining (See 'Further reading' and Chapter 13).

A FULL ENVIRONMENTAL AUDIT?

As we have said there has been much talk of audits. It is now becoming clear that the lead on what an environmental audit really is may emerge from the European Commission. Their proposed system defines such an audit as:

> A management tool comprising a systematic, documented, periodic and objective evaluation of how well organisations, managements and equipment are performing.

The aim of such audits is to:

- Facilitate corporate management and control of practices relevant to the environment.
- Improve company and public awareness of environmental performance.
- Identify possible improvements.
- Establish a basis for corporate environmental policy making.

An audit is also a valuable way of verifying and monitoring compliance with legislation and standards as well as being a basis for planning new training programmes. The targets above are in the EC draft 'Regulation Establishing a Community Environmental Auditing Scheme for Certain Industrial Activities', and when the final version is accepted it will become binding in all EC member states.

It now seems most likely that audits, at least at first, will be voluntary, but any company that wishes to be seen to be 'working greener' will certainly want to adopt the scheme early on. It also seems likely that, as the idea gains currency, so more and more companies will see the advantage. Thus a concept that was a novel idea just a few years ago is likely to become normal working practice in certain industries.

While these audits may not be legally binding they provide a useful way forward for any organisation that wishes to commit itself to sustainable working practices. Undertaking such a full audit will ensure that it stays ahead of those companies that will only move in this direction when forced to by legislation. It will also help a company keep track of how it is complying with and is being affected by new legislation from both parliament and the EC.

Auditing can be seen as having at least ten stages:

- Planning the audit, including deciding and allocating responsibilities and employing external advisors where applicable.
- A full review of the existing Corporate Environmental Protection Policy.
- An assessment of the organisation, management and equipment.
- Gathering of data.
- Evaluation of performance.
- Identification of areas for improvement.
- Reports to management.
- A follow-up statement by senior management.
- Consultation with staff in areas where changes are to take place.
- Implementation of recommendations.

Auditing is thus not a straightforward task to be undertaken once for publicity purposes. It is instead a way of ensuring that environmental policies are fully integrated into all aspects of the organisation's work and that those policies are being continually reviewed and taken forward.

For some organisations (such as a major local authority) the breadth of such a review may be so wide as to risk making it meaningless. It may also take so long as to be out-of-date by the time it is published. In this situation a Sustainable Work Action Group may wish to recommend that clearly separated units are audited separately in the context of an overall review.

Another way to introduce environmental audits is to establish an auditing process for all new projects: as they develop, their environmental impact is regularly assessed, while staff become used to working within a new discipline.

In addition to this comprehensive auditing an organisation may in time wish to commission specialised audits. These could include Compliance Audits (which look at how the organisation is meeting current legal standards), Health and Safety Audits (which should include an assessment of long-term occupational hazards) or Production Audits (these measure what goes in as materials and energy and what comes out in end products - the rest is waste or pollution).

Whatever the audit, it is essential that all staff are fully briefed and see the audit as a positive step forward for their section and the company. Full participation by staff is the basis for a successful audit that opens up new opportunities as well as highlighting problems to be tackled. Equally important is the production of a non-technical environmental statement, drawn up with and validated by the independent auditors, that can be released to the public or other interested bodies.

ENVIRONMENTAL IMPACT ASSESSMENTS

The third form of review is one that is becoming increasingly common. An Environmental Impact Assessment (EIA) would be carried out before a major development takes place and will provide planners with detailed information about how the proposal will affect the environment. EIAs are mandatory for all large developments in the USA and are now increasingly

---

Case Studies: Reviews in response to political change

Triplex Lloyd plc is an industrial engineering group serving the automotive, power and construction markets of Europe and North America. When the Environmental Protection Bill was going through parliament, Health, Welfare and Safety Adviser Hilary Marchant was asked to research its implications. Hilary pointed out: 'My research showed that the costs were going to be significant. I knew that the best advice to the company was to prepare for the coming of the Act sufficiently far in advance to enable decisions and plans to be made proactively rather than reactively.'

A technical committee was formed of staff from all the companies to enable employees to come to terms with acronyms such as BATNEEC and IPC. A review of waste management policy at all company sites was initiated. The review was done by Midland Research, a company within Triplex Lloyd whose brief was widened from materials testing to include reviews.

As Hilary said, 'The findings were astonishing. Some companies were paying for water, some did not. One company was throwing away a five-figure sum every month because it was an "essential part of the process" (it soon wasn't). Many companies were storing chemical "might-be's" - might be useful for this or that, or had been useful sometime - all unnecessary hazards to the environment.'

'Fourteen months later we know exactly where we have to target scarce resources. We have a very good idea how much it will all cost. We have an environmental policy which clearly defines accountability and responsibility.' To convey the results Triplex Lloyd and Midland Research held a seminar for all 30 of the company managing directors on the implication of the Environment Protection Act. This was so successful that they have now offered the package to companies outside the group.

demanded for the very largest developments in the UK (e.g. power stations).

Some companies have opposed this move, fearing that it will impede or even halt the proposal. Any company that is serious about its commitment to environmental quality should accept that some developments will be inappropriate and will cause too much damage: the sooner that this is discovered the better. As with any full-scale environmental audit, it is important that EIAs are carried out by reputable independent analysts.

GETTING YOUR REVIEWS DONE

There are many environmental consultants who can undertake reviews. There are considerably fewer who have the ability, experience and equipment necessary to carry out full audits or assessments. Environmental Data Services publish a list of consultants and more advice will be found in Appendix 1.

CHAPTER 12

WRITING A STRATEGY DOCUMENT

A strategy document should be an essential part of developing a sustainable work programme. It will outline what is being done and why, how the policies will be carried out and by whom. It can be read and agreed by all your staff and other 'stake-holders' (customers, suppliers, shareholders and neighbours) so that they know and understand what you're doing. It also ensures that important information is publicly available and not just in one person's head (or computer).

COMPILING THE DOCUMENT

(1) Set the goals and objectives for the report

As has been said before, setting goals and objectives is not an easy task, and to set goals for a company-wide strategy is much harder than setting goals for the first actions of the SWAG. The group who are working on the strategy document will need to put a lot of effort into ensuring the goals are suitable for the organisation. The group itself will need to be carefully selected and should contain representatives of the SWAG and the management. Use the same basic techniques outlined in Chapter 2 but be very aware of the need to consult extensively. Once the goals and objectives have been set they will keep the group focused on the purpose of the document.

(2) Plan the structure

Like all good writing, a strategy document needs a clear beginning, middle and end, so plan these stages and their purpose. A structure for a sustainable work document might be as follows:

Beginning Give a background or overview with reasons why sustainable work practices are desirable. State the goals for the strategy and describe what has already been done and what still needs to be done.

Middle This should be the core of the document, containing clear guidelines for staff, set out under appropriate headings, to help them work in sustainable ways.

End Succinctly review what you have covered, outline any areas that may need further research outside the immediate scope of the strategy, and request feedback on the document and suggestions for any changes.

(3) Use relevant headings

Appropriate headings guide readers and are invaluable aids to good communication. Consider your overall objective for the document and plan headings that reflect the objective. Ask yourself: 'What is the clearest way in which I can set this out so that people can easily follow the suggestions?'

Two possible structures are by materials or by departments. Thus a breakdown of headings in the middle section of a strategy document might be:

Strategies for work practices
- efficient use of energy
- minimising water usage
- the use of less toxic materials
- using less packaging
- machine maintenance

or:

Strategies for sections
- administrative office
- marketing section
- retail section
- warehouse
- purchasing section
- factory
- sales department

(4) Write simply and clearly

All writing should be easily understood. Do not use jargon or words that some people in the organisation may have difficulty understanding. This is particularly important when you are setting down guidelines or strategies.

If they are not clear, there is no chance that they will be followed.

- Use short sentences.

The maximum sentence length should be about 15-20 words. Each sentence should cover just one thought or idea.

- Use positive action-oriented words.

Research has shown that people understand statements more easily if they are couched in positive terms. Consider the following statements:

Negative: Do not throw paper away after it has been used.
Positive: Put used paper in the recycling boxes.

Negative: Do not waste water by not turning off the tap.
Positive: Help save water by always turning off taps.

Negative: Do not leave lights on in empty rooms.
Positive: Switch off the light as you leave the room.

The positive, action-oriented statement gets straight into the issue and is easier to understand. For more examples see Chapter 15.

Case Study: The City of Heidelberg

The major section headings in the City of Heidelberg's Conservation Strategy Document are framed as questions:

  Part A: So what's it all about?
  Part B: What can we do?
  Part C: What next?

Each section is broken up into sub-sections. For example Part B uses headings worded as actions:

- Controlling pollution and conserving energy
- Improving city life
- Travelling around without cars
- Protecting our natural assets
- Caring for companion animals
- Enriching leisure and conserving heritage
- Encouraging community involvement

Each sub-section is again split. 'Improving city life' has sub-headings dealing with particular aspects of city life:

- Arterial roads
- Residential street management
- Streetscapes
- Shopping centres
- Industrial areas

(5) Keep the document concise

More written documents would achieve their aim if they were not so long-winded. People simply get bored reading them. So keep the document as succinct as possible. Say what needs to be said and then stop.

(6) End on a positive note

You will want this document to be used as a basis for action, so make sure that you keep up the impetus right until the end. Conclude by bringing out the main points that you want the reader to remember and then request that people give you suggestions on changes to be made. You could even include a tear-out questionnaire for readers to fill in and return to you.

(7) Later revisions

This should not be a document 'cast in stone'. As with any strategy it should be flexible enough to take changing circumstances into account. As you learn more about sustainable ways of working you will certainly want to revise the document. Comments that you receive from readers are an important part of this process. Asking for feedback also helps the users of the document to feel that they are part of the process of producing it.

(8) Production of the document

This is a document that should be referred to regularly, so make sure that it stands out and looks attractive. It is not just a glorified internal memorandum! Get it well-designed and it should go without saying that it should be printed on recycled paper (heavy quality) with a cover that will withstand plenty of handling.

(9) Launching the strategy

If you've done your work well this will be a document that your organisation should be proud of. It gives you an opportunity to publicise both the idea of sustainable work and what your organisation is doing about it. So give the document the exposure it deserves!

Arrange a launch as you would for any major new product or service so that everyone knows about it. Invite all those who are 'stake-holders' in the organisation as well as community leaders and councillors, the local press, representatives of local environmental groups and other relevant people. Make sure that they get copies to take away and digest. This is an important occasion so make the most of it.

CHAPTER 13
GOING FORWARD INFORMED

For those who want to take it further there are plenty of places to get help, although this may not at first be obvious. The 1991 Booksellers' Association catalogue, *Books for Business*, lists over 140 books, of which just one touches on environmental issues!

Some of those who can help are environmental groups who can provide information or support, some are bodies created specifically to work with certain sectors while still others are long-standing bodies who have responded to environmental concern by producing relevant material.

Most environmental groups are supported largely by voluntary donations. They have very limited resources and therefore focus their work on achieving policy change at a parliamentary level. This means that they are not a good source of detailed advice on 'working greener' but they are usually well-informed and up-to-date on policy issues both in the UK and the EC.

Most of the national organisations have networks of voluntary local groups who may be able to supply speakers for meetings or offer basic practical advice. This can be very useful in the early stages of establishing your SWAG. Some organisations, both nationally and locally, are suspicious of approaches from commercial companies. This is due to the way in which a number of major polluting companies have attempted to deflect criticism by sponsoring environmental initiatives, and this may make closer working difficult, even for those companies with good reputations.

To build such links it is essential that companies listen to the concerns of the local groups and look for common ground (see Chapter 14) and do not attempt to impose their own agenda.

Some of the organisations who are specifically geared to provide useful advice are listed below:

Business in the Environment
BITE was launched in 1990 by Business in the Community with the support of HRH Prince Charles. They produced a useful video and an

excellent introductory book entitled *Your business and the environment - an executive guide*. This has been followed with a new publication *Your business and the environment - a D-I-Y review for companies* (due to be published summer 1991, price £24.95). This has been prepared by Coopers & Lybrand Deloitte and claims to be a workbook 'around which you can build your own review'. They can also put you in touch with other organisations who might be able to help. BITE moved in 1991 to 5 Cleveland Place, London SW1Y 6JJ.

Centre for Environment and Business in Scotland (CEBIS)
CEBIS is a new advice centre for Scottish businesses. They are based at 6 Scotland Street, Edinburgh EH3 6PS.

The Environment Council
The Environment Council has a membership of some 30 environmental groups including WWF and the National Trust but is run as an independent company and sees itself as a forum for discussion and the interchange of ideas. In 1989 it launched the Business and Environment Programme. Companies who subscribe to this receive regular in-depth mailings on a range of issues, while the main work of the programme is a series of seminars, briefings and conferences on specific issues. The programme may be one of the best ways for any company to come to grips with major environmental issues. The Council is now launching an Associate Membership scheme for individuals working on environmental matters in any sector. This will focus on developing ideas on mediation and conflict resolution. For full details write to: The Environment Council, 80 York Way, London N1 9AG (tel 071 278 4736).

Environmental Groups
Britain has an enormous range of environmental groups, including such well-known names as Friends of the Earth (FoE), Greenpeace, and the World Wide Fund for Nature (WWF). All these groups provide information to the public in varying degrees but few have the resources to provide the detailed information that a company might need.

FoE produce the *Environmental Charter for Local Government* (see below) and also have two technical manuals. *The Good Wood Manual* is aimed at designers and architects looking to specify alternatives to non-renewable tropical hardwoods, and a similar guide has recently been launched that details the various alternatives to peat for gardeners and landscapers. For details write to FoE, 26 Underwood Street, London N1 7JQ. They also produce a wide range of technical briefings that will be of use to specialists in areas such as air pollution. *The Green Diary* (produced each year by FoE, available in bookstores around Christmas) has one of the best listings of environmental groups, while *The Green Pages* has more detailed information (see 'Further reading').

The World-Wide Fund for Nature has extensive experience of working with companies, mostly on sponsorship. They have produced a book entitled *The Environmental Audit*, price £20, written by John Elkington of Sustainability. WWF are at Panda House, Weyside Park, Godalming, Surrey GU7 1XR.

Greenpeace have recently launched a bi-monthly publication *Greenpeace Business* aimed to carry their message and explain their approach to the business community. For subscription details write to Steve Walshaw, Greenpeace, Canonbury Villas, London N1.

The Royal Society for Nature Conservation, leading the development of the major 'Environment City' initiative in Leicester, have produced *Greening Business Premises*. This is aimed at businesses and at local groups who may be asked to advise businesses. It is a good practical guide to nature conservation and tree planting etc. around workplaces. It costs £5 inc. p&p from RSNC Publications, Witham Park, Lincoln LN5 7JR.

The Conservation Trust
The Trust is a long-standing educational charity that provides a wide range of educational materials on environmental matters. They have produced *Business and the Environmental Challenge* (see 'Further reading'). They are now intending to offer advice and information to managers and are developing a resource base for this. Basic advice is free, while more detailed inquiries may be charged for. For more information contact The Conservation Trust, National Environmental Education Centre, George Palmer Site, Northumberland Avenue, Reading, Berkshire RG2 7PW.

Environmental Concern Centre in Europe (ECCE)
ECCE is an example of a body founded as a result of industry's response to growing environmental concern. Its membership includes IBM UK, Rosehaugh PLC, the Ove Arup Partnership, the Tioxide group and several law firms. They say they are 'open to any company that is concerned about the managed environment and which has a demonstrable willingness to reduce damage to it'. The aim is to create an industrial self-help group in which members can discuss policy and ideas. ECCE functions as an information exchange and also organises seminars and conferences. Contact ECCE at 18 Victoria Park Square, London E2 9PF.

Sustainability
Sustainability came to prominence as a different sort of environmental group with the publication of *The Green Consumer Guide* in 1988. Since then they have produced a range of other material, most recently a pamphlet entitled *The Green Collar Worker* and a book by the founder John Elkington, Peter Knight and Julia Hailes, *The Green Business Guide* (see 'Further reading'). They also offer a review and auditing service. Sustainability, Peoples Hall, 91-97 Freston Road, London W11.

The Confederation of British Industry (CBI)
The CBI has produced a range of environmental publications. These include booklets on environmental auditing, on the greenhouse effect and energy efficiency, waste management, and a code of practice on archaeological investigations for mineral operators. Contact their environmental unit at CBI, Centre Point, 103 New Oxford Street, London WC1A 1DU.

The Department of Trade and Industry (DTI)
The DTI has established an environmental helpline which any organisation can ring for help or advice. The number is 0800 585794. For more information on this and other DTI services see Chapter 10.

The Department of Energy (DEn)
The Energy Efficiency Office within the DEn has a network of Regional Energy Efficiency Officers who can offer advice. For details of these and of their publications contact The Energy Efficiency Office, Department of Energy, Eland House, Stag Place, London SW1E 5DH.

The International Chamber of Commerce (ICC)
The ICC has produced a *Business Charter for Sustainable Development*. This document is not particularly radical but aims to be a 'basic framework of reference'. It has received widespread international support. The ICC is based at 38 Cours Albert 1er, 75008 Paris, France.

The British Library
The British Library runs an Environmental Information Service. For details write to 25 Southampton Buildings, London WC2 1DU.

INFORMATION FOR LOCAL GOVERNMENT

The first detailed guide to environmental action for local authorities was the Friends of the Earth 'Environmental Charter for Local Government'.

This comprehensive document looked at all aspects of local authority work and came out with 193 recommendations for positive action in areas as diverse as social services and economic development as well as more straightforwardly environmental departments.

A number of councils have adopted it in its entirety and time will tell how many manage to implement all its recommendations. Others have taken small parts of it, leading to somewhat weaker policies. Although it is aimed at local authorities it would be of interest and use to any environmental policy co-ordinator in a large company as an example of across-the-board working.

The other key guide is *Environmental Practice in Local Government*, produced by the Association of District Councils, 26 Chapter Street, London SW1P 4ND. This costs £15 to local authorities (£22.50 to others). It is a newer guide and thus contains some more up-to-date case studies but some of the practice described is not particularly good.

INFORMATION FOR TEACHERS

There is a flood of material on environmental education and bodies such as the Council for Environmental Education and the National Environmental Education Centre can advise on this. Of special note is the material produced by WWF, who produce a comprehensive catalogue. The most relevant to this book is their loose-leaf file *Greening the Staffroom*, a guide for both teachers and governors which includes 'a comprehensive range of ideas and activities for staff development in environmental education'. Purchasers of the file (price £25.99) also get a 30-minute BBC video entitled 'Greening the Classroom'.

At the higher education level, the Committee of Directors of Polytechnics has produced a document entitled *Greening Polytechnics*. This has a range of useful information and is available through the CDP, Kirkman House, 12-14 Whitfield Street, London W1P 6AX.

INFORMATION FOR TRADE UNIONS

Trade unions have plenty of information on health and safety at work and are a major resource in dealing with dangerous pollution issues. The TUC has recently produced a guide to environmental action entitled *Greening the Workplace - a TUC guide to environmental policies and issues at work* (see 'Further reading'). If your workplace is unionised ask the union steward if she or he has a copy.

This looks at a number of issues including:

- questions for trade unions to ask management.
- integrating health and safety in environmental issues.
- environmental training.
- 'green rights' at work.
- green pension funds.

The 'green rights' that are being proposed include a number of topics that any employer interested in involving all staff in sustainable practices might wish to consider. These are:

- The right to know the environmental impact of products and processes.
- The right to be informed and consulted on environmental strategy.
- The right to involvement in reviews and audits.
- The right to training and to be involved in designing training programmes.
- The right without recrimination to refuse to do work on environmentally harmful projects.

For details see 'Further reading'. A number of individual unions now have detailed environmental policies.

FINDING OUT MORE

One of the most worrying aspects of taking a lead on environmental work for your organisation is a feeling that you 'don't know enough'. This is a very common feeling, although attempts to resolve it can result very rapidly in information overload, since there is no shortage of printed material available.

The key to staying well-informed is to balance information on the basic issues with current affairs and with an overview. Key issues will vary from company to company while current environmental affairs are dealt with in some of the national press and by a few important journals. *New Scientist* remains the best and most interesting magazine covering environmental issues seriously, while the Environmental Data Services (ENDS) *Bulletin* is absolutely essential reading for the environmental policy co-ordinator in any organisation.

The mainstream monthly *Green Magazine* approaches these issues in a less technical manner but is a useful barometer of public interest (it also keeps an eye open for 'green cons'). There are also various smaller newsletters, some expensive and business-oriented, others with a useful regional angle. See 'Further reading' for details of these magazines.

GETTING THE INFORMATION OUT

Being well-informed is, of course, of little value if the information is not put to use. If the SWAG or your environmental policy co-ordinator is gathering information in an organised manner, it is important that you also look at how that information is passed around the organisation. If time and resources allow, there are several ways in which you could do this:

- producing a monthly digest of environmental news relevant to the actions being taken in your organisation.
- circulating a folder of press clippings to key staff each week.
- getting agreement to include an 'environmental news' column in your in-house magazine or newsletter. This can show all staff how actions taken internally are being matched by developments elsewhere.

CHAPTER 14

POSITIVE ACTION FOR THE FUTURE

A number of companies have gone beyond merely changing themselves and have looked to create changes elsewhere. Some of these initiatives have been very successful and imaginative. These show that company concern for the environment need not stop at providing support for environmental groups but can extend to doing the work yourself.

GIVING AWAY MONEY

Sponsorship is a well-established way for companies to promote themselves while supporting external initiatives. Some sponsorship has come in for criticism when polluting companies have used it as a way of buying some dubious green credibility. For all that, most environmental organisations are permanently short of money and will welcome the support.

Sponsorship is thus a good way for a company to use money. It is certainly more productive than giving donations or advertising but it requires more work on the part of the company if the full benefits are to be reaped. Some ways of ensuring that sponsorship will work include:

- Think carefully about any proposed project. Look at its likely effects just as you would any initiative inside the company. If there are any doubts, raise them with the proposer or look elsewhere.
- Assess the opportunities for your organisation. Sponsorship is a two-way relationship, so make sure that you will get adequate publicity for your investment, and that it is publicity of a kind that you want and can work with.
- Look for innovative projects. Projects that are 'safe' (e.g. tree planting) will get less press coverage than something new, although the innovative scheme may need more work on your part.
- What else can your organisation offer? The Body Shop's donation of window spaces (see below) is an excellent way of using company assets for little or no cost to give a smaller organisation new exposure.

- Look for long-term projects (if you are sure you can fund them). These are often more productive and it is harder for voluntary groups to find funding for on-going work.
- Involve your workforce. Projects in areas where your organisation is based may offer the opportunity for active involvement by your staff. Even if they don't, look for projects that staff will notice as they go about their daily lives and see as another example of the company taking positive action.

You may on occasion wish to donate money to groups. One American company recently responded to environmental concern among its staff by agreeing to match, dollar for dollar, all their donations to one particular campaign group. This is just one way of going beyond a straight donation.

GETTING YOUR HANDS DIRTY

Many organisations encourage their staff to 'play together' as well as work together. While some damage woodlands by running around shooting paintballs at each other, other companies are offering their employees a chance to actually benefit the environment.

USING WHAT YOU'VE GOT

Organisations looking to work with voluntary groups may be able to offer some specific opportunity as a result of the work that the organisations

---

Case Study: Action by the staff

Computer giant IBM were one of the first companies to mention the word sustainable when they introduced their Sustainable Development programme in 1987. While this programme has focused on providing support for international development projects, the company has also developed other environmental actions ranging from phasing out CFCs in computer manufacture to combatting soil erosion on company-owned land.

At a local level in the UK they have encouraged the development of LEATs - Local Environment Action Teams - at all their company bases. Staff are encouraged to develop teams to do volunteer work with local conservation groups to improve the local environment. Eighteen of these projects exist: some are straightforward conservation work, while IBM in Edinburgh has helped develop a Scottish environmental database and the IBM Sub-Aqua Club has helped map and restore a marine nature trail.

does. This could be one way to help publicise the work of the group.

CLEANING UP YOUR OWN INDUSTRY

It is important that any company that wants to be seen to be progressive in its approach to environmental issues regards legal standards merely as a minimum target. Organisations looking to work to the highest standards will look to go beyond legal base-lines, and may wish to encourage others to do so as well.

WORKING IN THE COMMUNITY

Any organisation that has made a commitment to adopting principles of sustainable working should be finding ways to pass on the idea to other organisations in the area and help in educational programmes.

Organisations such as the Rotary Club or Zonta International can provide a valuable forum for discussion. Companies could offer to supply a speaker who could outline the new developments and pass ideas on to others. The Chamber of Commerce is another place where businesses can work together and share ideas and information. In Truro the local Chamber of Commerce recently affiliated to Friends of the Earth and has been able to co-operate in local ventures.

Local authorities also have a major role to play. As part of developing a local environmental strategy many have set up environmental forums where voluntary groups can meet and discuss issues with councillors and officers. Those that work best appear to be those that have a built-in reporting mechanism to the relevant local committees. Other organisations

---

Case Study: Store-based campaigns

The Body Shop is well known for its environmental policies but one particular innovation is worthy of note. In 1987 the Body Shop developed a formal partnership with Friends of the Earth and on six occasions over the next two years devoted a window in each of its stores for one week to a campaign poster and display. These included weeks on rainforests, ozone and recycling.

Special leaflets were produced and distributed both through the shops and through FoE's local groups, who were able to use this link to boost their local profile. More recently the Body Shop has run its own campaigns, including a very successful initiative aimed at persuading the Brazilian government to take steps to stop burning of the Amazon rainforest.

> **Case Study:** Campaigning for tougher standards
>
> Ecover is a small detergent company which has been selling a range of cleaning products with minimum environmental impact in the UK since 1981. In 1989 it launched a political campaign to tighten and improve standards throughout the detergent industry.
>
> Ecover produced a series of 'green papers' that have set out how the industry could progressively phase out the most polluting chemicals. To back up these proposals the company launched a series of initiatives. These included the unique step of promoting a bill in parliament which received the support of over 300 MPs of all parties.
>
> The company has also mounted a trailer-based exhibition on water pollution that toured Britain for six months, and it is now producing its own education pack for schools about water pollution and conservation. Ecover passes on information about these aspects of its work to consumers through a newsletter included inside packs of washing powder.

seeking to develop their policies might wish to discover whether they could join such bodies.

GOING BEYOND GREEN

The upsurge of interest in how green issues relate to business has led some people to look beyond the issues of development and environment towards a more holistic or spiritual perspective for business. In the USA organisations such as the World Business Academy are adopting ideas and approaches that show how traditional management ideas can be transformed into something far more positive. The traditional 'command and control' style of management is being seen as inadequate and new ideas are being adopted by even the most mainstream firms.

A new code of ethics for businesses appears to be emerging. One clear pointer to the future has been the Valdez Principles (see below). These represent a very broad front for action, including the appointment of an environmental representative to the board of directors. While they were seen as too progressive not long ago, the overall trend in the USA is clearly in their direction.

In Britain this movement has been slower but change is in the air. One document on the subject, *Ethics, Environment and the Company*, was produced by the Green Alliance and the IBE (Institute for Business Ethics) in 1990.

Most moves towards an ethical and holistic approach to business have been led by a range of individuals, many of whom are members of The

> **Case Study:** Launching a local campaign
>
> Another way forward is to set up a new body. In Southampton a new association has been launched to promote the greening of local industry. SIEnA (Solent Industrial Environment Association) was set up with the support of local councils, businesses and environmental groups. Its aims include promoting environmental awareness, the sharing and dissemination of knowledge in all fields of environmental concern, and the study of appropriate statutory requirements.
>
> It points out that there has been a huge growth in the number of conferences on environmental topics but adds: 'SIEnA is different. We bring the experts to Southampton so you don't have to travel. Most importantly we aim to deal with practical problems and practical solutions.'

> **Case Study:** From worker to associate
>
> A General Electric plant at Salisbury in the USA that manufactured electric circuit breakers hit problems in the mid-80s. The company responded with a complete re-organisation and a three-level workforce: associates, advisors and plant manager. The workforce - now 'associates' - is organised into self-managing teams that plan and hire as well as turn out the products. Elected facilitators and cross-functional committees involve the associates in major policy issues. Costs have been reduced by 30%, there has been a ten-fold drop in customer complaints and delivery dates have been cut from three weeks to three days. (Reported in *The McKinsey Quarterly*, Issue 1, 1991).

Business Network. This organisation has been running for about eight years, produces a newsletter and organises regular meetings with speakers. A recent series included the major environmental spokespeople for each political party, and international speakers are regularly featured. The Business Network has been very London-oriented but now plans to launch regional networks. Membership is £35 a year. Contact The Business Network, 18 Well Walk, Hampstead, London NW3 1LD.

THE VALDEZ PRINCIPLES

In 1989 a US umbrella group, the Coalition for Environmentally Responsible Economies (CERES), which included conservation groups such as the Sierra Club and Friends of the Earth along with the Social Investment Forum and other bodies, launched a series of ten principles for business.

Companies that sign up are asked to file an annual CERES report, explaining and discussing their achievements in complying with the Principles. They are also asked to pay a small fee, based on their revenue (e.g. a company with an income of $10 to $50 million pays $500 a year).

The founding group stated that: 'Our intent is to create a voluntary mechanism of corporate self-governance that will maintain business practices consistent with the goals of sustaining our fragile environment for future generations, within a culture that respects all life and honours its interdependence.'

The principles are a summary of much of what has been discussed in this book, and make it clear that 'working greener' is a permanent process. They provide a long-term target for any organisation that really believes in a sustainable future for humanity on this planet. The Valdez Principles are:

(1) *Protection of the biosphere*
We will minimise and strive to eliminate the release of any pollutant that may cause environmental damage to the air, water or earth or its inhabitants. We will safeguard habitats in rivers, lakes, wetlands, coastal zones and oceans and will minimise contributions to the greenhouse effect, depletion of the ozone layer, acid rain or smog.

(2) *Sustainable use of natural resources*
We will make sustainable use of renewable natural resources, such as water, soils and forests. We will conserve non-renewable natural resources through efficient use and careful planning. We will protect wildlife habitats, open spaces and wilderness, while preserving biodiversity.

(3) *Reduction and disposal of water*
We will minimise the creation of waste, especially hazardous waste, and wherever possible recycle materials. We will dispose of all wastes through safe and responsible methods.

(4) *Wise use of energy*
We will make every effort to use environmentally safe and sustainable energy sources to meet our needs. We will invest in approved energy efficiency and conservation in our operations. We will maximise the energy efficiency of what we produce and sell.

(5) *Risk reduction*
We will minimise the environmental, health and safety risks to our employees and the communities in which we operate by employing safe technologies and operating procedures and by being constantly prepared for emergencies.

(6) *Marketing of safe products and services*
We will sell products or services that minimise adverse environmental impacts and that are safe as consumers commonly use them. We will inform customers of the environmental impacts of our products and services.

(7) *Damage compensation*
We will take responsibility for any harm that we cause to the environment by making every effort to restore the environment and to compensate those persons who are adversely affected.

(8) *Disclosure*
We will disclose to our employees and to the public incidents relating to our operations that cause environmental harm or pose health or safety hazards. We will disclose potential environmental, health or safety hazards posed by our operations, and we will not take any action against employees who report any condition that creates a danger to the environment or poses health or safety hazards.

(9) *Environmental directors and managers*
We will commit management resources to implement the Valdez Principles, to monitor and report our implementation efforts, and to sustain a process to ensure that the Board of Directors and Chief Executive Officer are kept informed of and are fully responsible for all environmental matters. We will establish a Committee of the Board of Directors with responsibility for environmental affairs. At least one member of the Board of Directors will be a person qualified to represent environmental interests that come before the company.

(10) *Review and annual audit*
We will conduct and make public an annual self-evaluation of our progress in implementing these principles and in complying with applicable laws and regulations throughout our world-wide operations. We will work towards the creation of independent environmental audit procedures which we will complete annually and make available to the public.

CHAPTER 15

ACTIONS FOR EVERY WORKPLACE

Throughout this book there have been ideas and recommendations for positive actions. To pull it all together, here is a summary of practices that should be adopted by organisations that wish to develop sustainable work practices.

GENERAL

- Set goals for your workplace to be a model for sustainable work practices.
- Form a Sustainable Work Action Group.
- Arrange for walk-through reviews in each department.
- Create a culture within the organisation that the environment matters and that 'sustainable work works'.
- Arrange training sessions and seminars for staff on sustainable work issues.
- Devise a strategy plan to develop a company environmental policy and ways to implement it.
- Allow time off from normal duties for key staff to meet in a Sustainable Work Action Group.
- Incorporate care for the environment as a key part of the organisation's striving for 'total quality'.
- Keep all staff informed of any sustainable work initiatives within the organisation and of similar projects elsewhere.
- Hold an open staff meeting to discuss the 3 Rs: reduce, reuse and recycle.
- Encourage employee incentive schemes for suggestions for sustainable work practices.
- Promote environmental initiatives by advising clients, local authorities and the public through local and regional media and through all company products and brochures.

- Support local community initiatives to protect and improve the environment.
- Begin a tree planting programme around buildings and/or in the locality.
- Make contact with other organisations and groups to share the knowledge gained from working in sustainable ways.
- Conform to all environmental protection guidelines and legislation and examine ways in which the organisation could progress beyond these minimum standards.
- Support moves towards an open 'freedom of information' system for the UK.
- Let your MP and MEP know that your company fully endorses proposals to reduce greenhouse gas emissions in line with international agreements.

ENERGY

- Act on the results of walk-through reviews to take the first steps to cut down on waste of energy.
- Arrange for an energy audit by an external consultant if your workplace is a large user of energy.
- Ensure that all rooms are draughtproofed.
- Use light coloured walls, ceilings, floor coverings and furnishings to reflect light and make rooms brighter.
- Launch a programme to replace standard light bulbs with low-wattage bulbs.
- Keep lighting fixtures and bulbs free of dust to ensure maximum efficiency.
- Encourage members of the SWAG to keep a check on whether their parts of the building are over-heated.
- Check thermostats weekly to ensure maximum efficiency.
- When buying any new equipment assess its energy efficiency and take this into account in making a choice.
- Do not permanently heat or cool rooms that are infrequently used, such as conference or meeting rooms.
- Make sure all electrical equipment is regularly maintained.
- Incorporate passive solar design into any new or renovated buildings.
- Set the highest standards for energy efficiency in any products that you manufacture.

EQUIPMENT, MATERIAL AND PRODUCTS

- Ensure all equipment is well maintained and serviced to prevent any escape of fumes or pollutants.
- Ensure that all operating equipment is in well-ventilated rooms.
- Have refrigerators and air conditioners checked regularly by qualified service staff, and discuss with suppliers how they intend to replace any CFCs in use in the equipment.
- Phase out all CFC use within the organisation as rapidly as possible.
- Contact a supplier of re-inked printer ribbons for computers and set up a contract for them to service and supply ribbons.
- Check the labels of all substances used by the organisation. Look for less toxic alternatives to any hazardous materials currently in use.
- Disallow the introduction of new hazardous materials.
- Buy locally-produced materials wherever possible to cut indirect energy use and to support local businesses.
- Support 'fair trade' initiatives designed to help developing countries and insist that your own importing of materials conforms to these guidelines.
- Purchase products made using recycled materials wherever possible.
- Set up recycling systems within the organisation.
- Purchase only solvents and detergents that have minimum environmental impact.
- Phase out the use of disposable plastic cups throughout the organisation.
- Avoid all use of tropical hardwoods and products from endangered species.
- Replace aerosols with pump action sprays.
- Follow developments on plans to introduce 'eco-labelling' schemes. When this starts, look to buy products that have received a label. Ensure that all products manufactured by your organisation can, if appropriate, receive such a symbol.
- Demand that all plastic products that your organisation purchases are coded to assist recycling efforts.
- Insist that suppliers use natural or recycled fibres as packaging materials.

PAPER

- Set up a paper recycling programme.
- Organise a 'save paper' competition for suggestions on how to cut paper waste most effectively.

- Begin writing replies by hand on the bottom of internal memos and letters and encourage others to do the same.
- Review paper purchasing policy and use 100% recycled and unbleached paper wherever possible.
- Reuse envelopes wherever possible; produce envelope reuse labels with the company logo and address on.
- Install an electronic mail system and use it wherever possible.
- Always ask whether a phone call would do instead of a letter.
- Inspect all mailing lists and reduce the number of names on them.
- Adopt a policy of returning unwanted, unsolicited mail to the sender.
- Review organisation policy on report, letter and memo format and revise policy to save space and paper.
- Produce pre-printed action slips for use in the organisation, with complement slips and memo forms.
- Institute a policy of double-sided photocopying as standard and ensure that your copiers are good enough to handle this.
- Ensure that all paper/card packaging is recycled.
- Use unbleached recycled toilet paper throughout the organisation.
- Print all company publications, brochures and reports on recycled paper and highlight this in each one.

TRANSPORT

- Organise a 'get fit' campaign which includes walking, using public transport and using the stairs.
- Offer incentives to staff to use public transport.
- Arrange a company bus to transport employees to and from principal public transport points.
- Arrange the provision of convenient and secure cycle parking facilities.
- Offer cyclists a space to change and shower before work.
- Set up company car pooling arrangements.
- Discourage the practice of supplying company cars except where strictly necessary.
- Devise salary packages that do not include company cars.
- Develop a company policy that only one model of company car will be supplied, and that this will have a catalytic converter.
- Ensure that all company cars are fine tuned and serviced regularly.
- Encourage increases in fuel efficiency of motor vehicles by offering incentives.
- Conduct seminars for staff on safe and energy-efficient driving.

- Set 'engine running' time limits for delivery vehicles.
- Ensure that all transport of dangerous materials or wastes is handled so as to avoid any pollution.
- Assess the way in which freight is transported by your organisation and consider alternative methods, notably rail transport.
- Consider running organisation vehicles on liquid petroleum gas (LPG).
- Lobby for better rail and bus transport systems for your staff and your goods.
- Use cycle couriers rather than cars or motor cycles.

WATER

- If you are a large user of water, discuss auditing your use with your local water company.
- Check all taps and pipes for leaks.
- Encourage staff to report all leaks and replace leaking washers on taps etc. as soon as they are reported.
- Ensure that no oils, fats or solids enter, or are likely to enter, any stormwater drain system.
- Install twin-flush toilets during rebuilding or refurbishment programmes.
- Install 'Cistermiser' controls on urinals.
- Put a 'toilet dam' (or a sealed plastic bag of water) in your toilet cisterns.
- Do not use toilets as ash-trays or waste-baskets (every flushed cigarette butt wastes ten litres of water in a standard toilet).
- Use brooms, mops and buckets of water for cleaning rather than hoses.
- Use trigger attachments on hoses to cut water loss while moving hoses around.
- Arrange a system where uncontaminated waste water can be used for landscape watering.
- Use mulches around plants or trees (this can save over half the water loss through evaporation).
- Water the roots of plants, not the leaves.
- Water plants and trees thoroughly when needed but less frequently.
- Use a timer on any garden watering system.
- Investigate new ways of handling waste water.
- Report any water pollution incidents to your local water company and your local council.

WASTE

- Reduce waste by buying and using materials that can be reused or recycled and that are durable and repairable.
- Take responsibility for all wastes that emanate from the workplace.
- Discuss waste minimisation plans with your local waste authority and ensure that all hazardous waste collection procedures are operating to the highest standards.
- Keep an up-to-date official record of the location, quantity and nature of any toxic materials used and all hazardous waste materials.
- Practice in-plant pollution control and waste treatment to reduce or eliminate the need for off-site treatment.
- Invest in technology that will provide the ability to deal with hazardous waste on site.
- Comply strictly with all codes and regulations that cover waste.
- Devise ways to reuse all packaging materials that come into the workplace.
- Participate in any local recycling schemes and lobby your council for improved recycling facilities.
- Keep up-to-date on new cleaner technologies as they become available.
- Get involved with the development of new codes of practice for waste minimisation and recycling.
- Investigate the use, in every part of the workplace, of materials that are less toxic and create less waste and pollution.
- Investigate the substitution of recycled products for raw materials to reduce the burden on natural resources.

APPENDIX 1
FURTHER READING

GENERAL READING:

Our Common Future - The Report of the World Commission on Environment and Development, Oxford University Press, £6.95. Generally known as the 'Brundtland Report', and unashamedly described by its publishers as 'the most important document of the decade', it is still a key book for anyone who wants to understand the issues.

How to Be Green, John Button, Century Hutchinson, £4.99. This is perhaps the best of the guides for individuals and is a good starting point for anyone who wants an overview of all aspects of 'being green'.

Green Pages, John Button, Macdonald Optima, £9.99. This comprehensive catalogue of all things green may on first glance seem a little too 'alternative' for many organisations but it remains a very useful source of contacts and ideas and is an important reference text.

Blueprint for a Green Economy, David Pearce *et al.*, Earthscan Books, £6.95. The first book to actually take a practical look at the economic realities of sustainable development. The book has caused considerable debate within environmental circles - many question the extent to which almost arbitrary values can be given to irreplaceable natural resources. Its successor, *Greening the World Economy*, is also stimulating reading.

EEC Environmental Policy and Britain, Nigel Haigh, Longman, £38.50. The definitive guide to this increasingly important aspect of environmental policy. A second edition came out in 1990, but with constant changes on the agenda, it may be worth enquiring about the third edition, due out in 1992.

Save the Earth, Jonathon Porritt, Dorling Kindersley. A major overview of environmental issues around the globe, with contributions from many well-known figures. Anyone confused by the sheer scope of the environmental debate should find this a good place to start.

Small is Beautiful, E.F. Schumacher, Abacus, £3.99. This book was one of the cornerstones on which the environmental movement was built, although Schumacher's career was strictly in the business world. The book's examination of what is truly appropriate will be of interest to anyone who wants to look beyond immediate environmental concerns.

C for Chemicals, Mike Birkin and Brian Price, Green Print, £4.99. This looks at hundreds of chemicals in use around the home and in the workplace and assesses their hazardousness and points to alternatives. A good starting point for any manager who wants to understand what the technical advisers are saying.

P for Pollution, Brian Price, Green Print, £5.99. Another straightforward and authoritative guide that looks at pollutants in the environment and their effects on humans and other life. This new book includes a chapter on legal controls.

State of the World Report: this is produced by the Worldwatch Institute (USA). The annual reports from the prestigious Worldwatch Institute are a surprisingly well-kept secret in Britain but are essential reading for anyone who wants to keep in touch with important developments around the world. Worldwatch also produce a regular series of briefing documents on specific subjects. Their publications are available in the UK through Books for a Change (see below).

The Global Consumer - produced by *New Consumer* magazine, Gollancz Books. This will examine the role of market leader companies in certain areas in encouraging fair and equitable trade with developing nations. This will be the first British book on this important area of green concern.

GREEN BUSINESS

Business and the Environment, Georg Winter, McGraw Hill, £14.95. This was the first book that showed managers how to start cleaning up their act. It was produced for European Year of the Environment (1987) and is now slightly out of date but remains one of the most comprehensive reviews of the subject. Georg Winter has developed an 'Integrated System of Environmentalist Business Management' that is known as the Winter Model. It has been said that this is more suitable for the German 'compliance-oriented culture' than for the current situation in Britain, but it remains a standard work in the field.

Green Business: Hope or Hoax?, edited by Judith and Christopher Plant, Green Books, £5.99. As the title suggests this US book is rather more critical than some of those mentioned here. It is well worth reading for the examples of progressive practice that it highlights and for its irreverent '50 difficult things you can do to save the earth'.

Business in the Environment - An Executive Guide. £5 from Business in the Environment. As an introduction for sceptical business people this is excellent. Unsurprisingly it tends to sing the virtues of a voluntary approach but it is still probably the best summary of the central areas of concern.

The Green Business Guide, John Elkington, Peter Knight and Julia Hailes, Gollancz, £16.99. John Elkington, founder of Sustainability, has been at the forefront of business involvement in environmental action. This new book provides more ideas and guidelines for the greener manager.

Green Reporting - Accountancy and the Challenge of the Nineties, edited by David Owen, Chapman Hall (forthcoming). This overview will examine the role of accountants in organisations as interests beyond the maximisation of profits comes increasingly to the fore.

Changing Corporate Values, produced by *New Consumer* magazine, Kogan Page, £48. This describes itself as 'a guide to social and environmental policy and practice in Britain's top companies' and is just that. 128 companies are profiled in depth, with descriptions in categories that include environmental impact and action, women's advancement, power and influence and others. Not cheap but very comprehensive at 638 pages.

Costing the Earth, Frances Cairncross, Economist Books, £16.99. An extremely detailed look at the whole issue of environmental management with the thoroughness and political analysis that one would expect from *The Economist*.

Greening Business, John Davis, Blackwell, £18.99. John Davis recently retired after many years of experience both in commercial management and in setting up Local Enterprise Trusts. He is a keen supporter of Schumacher and his book is described by Sir Peter Parker as relating the 'formidable realities of environmental policy for industry' to issues such as company law, democracy at work and managing change.

All the above can be obtained through good bookshops or from Books for a Change, who offer a comprehensive mail order service. Send a large SAE for a catalogue to: Books for a Change, 52 Charing Cross Road, London WC2H 0BB (tel 071 836 2315; fax 071 497 1036).

The TUC *Environmental Manual for Workplaces* is available from the Publications Department, TUC, Great Russell Street, London WC1 price £4.

Going Green - A Starter Pack for Business. Sponsored by the London Borough of Ealing and prepared by Green Audits, it costs £50. This 84-page manual is aimed very specifically at a manager who wishes to initiate changes in the workplace through a review. It contains a number of photocopiable sheets for passing on to section heads along with a review planner and timetable. It also has a useful legal overview. Available from Ealing Council Economic Development Unit, Perceval House, 14-16 Uxbridge Road, London W5 2HL.

Business and the Environmental Challenge - A Guide for Managers, Colin Hutchinson, The Conservation Trust, £9.50. A brief and straightforward guide with examples and guidelines. Available from The Conservation Trust, N.E.E.C., George Palmer Site, Northumberland Avenue, Reading, Berkshire RG2 7PW.

A complete listing and review of EC environmental legislation, including full information about all Directives etc., has been produced by Environmental Policy Consultants, a lobby group. For full details and price write to EPC, 33 Brailsford Road, London SW2 2TB.

JOURNALS

Environmental Data Services Bulletin (ENDS). This monthly bulletin is, as said elsewhere, essential. It provides the best coverage of what is really happening on environmental issues right across the spectrum. It pulls few punches and is well aware of pressure group positions on key issues. Subscription is £180 a year (introductory rate for new subscribers £90) - details from ENDS, Unit 24 Finsbury Business Centre, Bowling Green Lane, London EC1R 0NE.

Environment Business. A fortnightly newsletter aimed very much at businesses with active environmental concerns and containing increasing amounts of useful hard information. It is produced by Information for Industry, 521 Old York Road, London SW18 1TG.

Environmental Impact. A detailed monthly specialist newsletter, produced by Industry and Environment Associates. Good on audits, waste and energy issues. Price £283.70 (inc. VAT) per year which also allows you to request press clippings on featured issues and to access some of their facilities. Subscribers also receive their International Environment Directory. Details from IEA, 77 Temple Sheen Road, East Sheen, London SW14 7RS.

Integrated Environmental Management is a new monthly, aiming to cover all aspects of environmental management issues for business and the academic community. Details and rates from Anna Rivers, Blackwell Scientific Publications, Osney Mead, Oxford OX2 0EL.

European Environment. Described as 'the practical journal of environment policy and practice for Europe in the 1990s' this covers what is clearly going to be a crucial area for all policy makers. Published bi-monthly and priced very reasonably at £38, details from European Environment, European Research Press, P.O. Box 75, Shipley, W. Yorks BD17 6EZ.

Environment Digest is a useful and authoritative monthly review of key issues world-wide. Subscriptions are £38/yr for organisations, £19/yr for individuals, and £15/yr for students and the unwaged. Details from Environmental Digest, Panther House, 38 Mount Pleasant, London WC1X 0AP.

Green Magazine is produced monthly by Northern & Shell Publishers. *New Scientist* is a weekly from IPC. Both should be available at any good newsagent.

Most environmental groups produce newsletters, usually on a quarterly basis. These vary in content and style but will often cover up-to-the-minute policy issues. There are a number of smaller magazines, amongst which are *Green News*, based in the Avon area with coverage of regional and national issues and *The Globe*, based in Sheffield with excellent coverage of northern environmental matters.

APPENDIX 2
TEN WAYS TO SAVE ON PACKAGING

(1) Recycle your packaging
Any packaging materials that arrive at your workplace should be reused when you send out other packages. This includes the cardboard boxes and the envelopes as well as the internal packing materials.

(2) Use recycled materials
All boxes and envelopes should be made of recycled materials. Shredded paper (perhaps those types of paper that cannot be recycled) is a good alternative to foam 'peanuts' for many purposes. Small shredders are widely available. Some companies used crumpled-up computer paper - which could be recycled by the recipient.

(3) Think natural
The idea of using pop-corn as packaging filler may seem slightly eccentric but it has the same protective qualities as foam peanuts and is entirely biodegradable.

(4) Go naked!
Products that used to be sold 'au naturel' - without any packaging (e.g. ballpoint pens or small tools such as hammers or screwdrivers) are now all too often sold in blister packs. Apart from making it harder for the customer to inspect the goods the only other advantage seems to be to give the vendor a place to put a bar code. Is this really necessary?

(5) Use paper rather than plastic
Do it wherever you can! Consider also cellophane which is fully degradable.

(6) Make it refillable, reusable and recyclable
In other words, think about all aspects of your packaging and how it could be improved.

(7) Make less packaging an art form
Devise your minimal packaging strategy in such a way that it becomes a selling point for your product.

(8) Support returnable bottles
A recent survey showed 84% support for returnable bottles. The manufacturers say the supermarkets won't use them: the supermarkets say it's the manufacturers. Who's fooling whom?

(9) Pressurise your suppliers
If you're going to improve your packaging, why shouldn't your suppliers? You're their customer so use some of that green consumer pressure.

(10) Don't stop there!
As you become waste and over-packaging conscious, keep the new ideas coming. Encourage staff to look one step further.

APPENDIX 3
TEN STEPS TO A GREENER OFFICE

(1) Cut the waste
That means an office paper recycling scheme, can collection points and an end to plastic coffee cups (you know it all makes sense!). If there's open space and gardens around your workplace how about a composting scheme?

(2) No more 'sick building syndrome'
It's not just an excuse - we've all been in buildings that are far better places to work in than others. Improve ventilation and use of natural light for starters. Bring plants into the office (but don't use pesticides on them).

(3) Watch those computer terminals
The arguments continue about radiation from VDUs. While computers emit very little high frequency ionising radiation (the radiation that comes from radioactive materials or X-rays) they do emit non-ionising radiation as a result of the transformers and high voltages used inside the TV screens.

The evidence is building about the health risks. Some will dismiss them (but remember that only 25 years ago it was common practice to X-ray pregnant women, and the people who challenged that were dismissed as cranks). The 'precautionary principle' is coming in for new processes - apply it here! Minimise your exposure, both to the front of your screen and (especially) to the back of your neighbour's unit. Some companies are painting the inside of their VDU casing with a metallic paint to absorb much of the radiation, and fine mesh screens are available for the display screen.

(4) Watch those printers and copiers too!
Laser printers and most copiers emit ozone gas while in normal operation. It's at very low levels (and gas masks are not needed!), but it does make sense to minimise the pollution. Some people are highly sensitive to ozone and it will attack anyone's mucous membranes (in the nose and eyes). Exposure to ozone breaks down the outer layers of the membranes and makes the exposed person more susceptible to viruses and bacteria, causing colds etc.

So keep those machines in a well-ventilated space. Check your laser printer air filters. Don't have a well-used laser printer right next to your desk. If possible, site printers and copiers near extractor fans.

(5) And those printer ribbons and cartridges as well!
Toner cartridges can be refilled and reused (in Japan it's now a legal requirement) and ribbons for dot matrix and other printers can be re-inked. Ask your suppliers about cartridge re-filling (if they can't do it, ask why not!) and if you have a number of machines using ribbons consider getting a re-inker - it could save you hundreds of pounds a year. One firm who supply in the UK are MGA SoftCat (tel 0797 226601); many more are now appearing on the market.

(6) Cut the use of paper
Electronic mail and electronic faxes are the high-tech way; responding to memos with a handwritten note on the memo is low-tech but a lot cheaper and quicker. Once you start 'thinking paper' you'll be able to come up with other ways.

(7) Green and clean
Check those cleaning products. Look for the ones with the least environmental impact - become a critical consumer. Who needs air fresheners if the office is well ventilated?

(8) Spread the good ideas around
If your section comes up with a good idea, let the rest of the workplace know about it.

(9) Find out more
Environmental issues change fast. Keep up-to-date with the news and pass items of interest or concern around the office. Make contact with local environmental action groups and find out what's going on in the neighbourhood.

(10) And that's just for starters
As we've said elsewhere, 'working greener' is a process with no absolute end. So set targets, and when you've met them look for new ones - they won't be hard to find!

INDEX

accountants *13*
actions for every workplace *135-40*
Advanced Environmental Research Group *72*
aluminium cans *45*
architects *14*
Association of District Councils ADC *123*
d'Aquino, Thomas *29*

Bellamy, David *102*
biomass *68*
Blue Circle Group *91*
Blueprint for a Green Economy 2, *141*
Body Shop *81, 83, 127, 129*
'Books for a Change' mail order *143*
Booksellers' Association *120*
British Library *122*
British Telecom *4, 45*
British Wind Energy Association *67*
Brundtland, Gro Harlem *1, 2*
Brundtland Report 2, *141*
builders *14*
Building Research Establishment *75* Environmental Assessment (BREEAM) *76*
Business in the Community *119*
Business in the Environment *3, 110, 120, 142*
Business Network, The *131*
Button, John *141*

C for Chemicals 141
CFCs *61*
   recovery of *89*
carbon dioxide 'personal budgets' *82*
carbon dioxide emissions *60ff*
catalytic conferters *80*
Caird Group *6*

Centre for Alternative Technology *67*
chambers of commerce *129*
cleaning staff *14*
Coca Cola *47*
Combined Heat and Power (CHP) *66*
Commoner, Barry *44*
composting *45*
computer terminals *147*
Confederation of British Industry *122*
Conservation Trust *121*
Control of Pollution Act *3*
councillors *14*
council staff *14*
couriers, use of *85*
Cranfield School of Management *4*
critical path analysis *24*
cycling *83ff*

Department of Energy *59, 67-8, 72, 122*
Department of Trade and Industry *45, 68, 89, 101, 122*
Department of the Environment *96, 101*
Denver, John *10*
designers *15*
diesel cars *80*
Dow Chemicals *47, 88*
'driving sustainably' *82*

Ealing, London Borough of *143*
eco-labelling *96*
Ecological Trading Company *100*
ECOTEC *97*
Ecover *81, 130*
Elkington, John *122, 142*
energy conservation *64ff, 69ff*

actions for every workplace *136*
energy efficiency *59, 63ff*
  in buildings *71ff*
energy management *63*
engineers *15*
entertainment industry *15*
Environment Business newsletter *144*
Environment Concern Centre for Europe (ECCE) *121*
Environment Council *19, 120*
Environment Digest *144*
Environmental Audits *108, 110ff*
Environmental Data Services (ENDS) *Bulletin 87, 113, 124, 143*
environmental education *123*
Environmental Impact Assessment *112*
Environmental Management Options Scheme (DEMOS) *101*
Environmental Policy Consultants (EPC) *143*
Environmental Protection Act *87*
Environmental Protection Agency (EPA) *60*
environmental reviews *21, 108ff*
Environmental Technology Innovation Scheme (ETIS) *101*
Environmental Transport Association *81*
Envirosafe *17*
European Commission (EC) *97, 110, 143*

factory staff *15*
'Fair Trade Mark' *98*
Fort Sterling papers *57*
Friends of the Earth *45, 57, 62, 100, 120, 123, 129, 131*

gardeners *16*
General Electric *132*
glass recycling *43, 46*
global warming *59ff*
green 'cons' *125*
Green Alliance *130*
Green Magazine *124, 144*
Green News *144*

greenhouse effect (*see* global warming)
Greenpeace *120*
Green Print books *58*

hairdressers *16*
Harlow District Council *65*
Hazzard, Shirley *12*
heat pumps *66*
Heidelberg, City of *117*
Her Majesty's Inspectorate of Pollutions (HMIP) *92*
Heseltine, Michael *95*
HRH Prince Charles *1*

IBM *74, 121, 128*
Iceland Frozen Foods *90*
Industry & Environment Associates *144*
Institute of Directors *4*
Institute for Business Ethics *130*
Independent Waste Paper Processors Association (IWPPA) *57*
insulation *72*
International Chamber of Commerce (ICC) *122*
investment advisers *16*

Kelloggs *65*
kitchen staff *14*
Kwik Seal Products *65*

least cost energy planning *64*
Littlewoods Stores *98*
local government, information for *123*
  actions by *14, 72*

mailing lists *53*
Mailing Preference Service *54*
marketing staff *16*
McKinsey Quarterly 132
management, working with *26*
  role of *47ff*
Manchester Airport *66*
Mead, Margaret *19*
media staff *17*
medical staff *17*
methane *60*
Milland Fine Timber *100*

INDEX

Milton Keynes Energy Park 72, 74
Mowlem Engineering 66
Muir, John 106

National Rivers Authority (NRA) 92
natural gas 61
New Consumer 98, 142
New Scientist 61, 124, 144
newspapers 54
Next Retail 76
nitrous oxide 61
No Smoking policies 37
nuclear power 60

office staff 17
office, ten steps to a greener 147
Ouma, Joseph 11
Our Common Future see *Brundtland Report*

P for Pollution 142
packaging 47
   reduction 145
Packaging Week 47
paper recycling 54ff, 137
Paper Recycling Company, The 54
PaperRound 56
Pearce, David 2, 3, 141
Pilkington Glass 76
plastic cups 47, 147
plastics recycling 46
plumbers 17
'polluter pays' principle 3
Polytechnics, Committee of Directors of 123
Porritt, Jonathon 141
Pre-press Services 191
'precautionary principle' 3, 147
public relations staff 16
public transport 84ff
publishers 17, 57
purchasing officers 17

radiation from computer terminals 147
recycled materials, use of 58, 145
recycling 41, 44ff
   of aluminium 46
   of glass 46
   of paper 49, 54ff

   of plastics 46
   of toner cartridges 148
'Recycling City' 45
renewable energy 67ff
returnable bottles 147
Rocky Mountain Institute 60
Rotary Clubs 129
Royal Society for Nature Conservation (RSNC) 121
Ruskin, John 49

Sainsbury's 47
Schumacher E.F. 59
sick building syndrome 147
Sheffield 45
Sierra Club 106, 131
small business owners 18
solar power 67
Southampton Industry and Environment Association (SIEnA) 131
sponsorship 127
supermarket staff 18
Sustainability 121-2
'Sustainable Work Action Groups' 7, 19ff, 30, 55, 107-8, 111
Suzuki, David 87

teachers 18, 123
Thoreau, Henry 40
toner cartridge recycling 148
Toronto Conference on the Changing Atmosphere 59
tourist industry staff 18
trade unions, involvement of 20
Trades Union Congress (TUC) 20, 97, 123, 143
Traidcraft 98
training of staff 108
transport 79ff, 138
   of products 85
'Total Environmental Quality' 41
Triplex Lloyd plc 112

University
   of Edinburgh 75
   of Strathclyde 76
unleaded petrol 80

Valdez Principles 131

vehicle hire *85*
visual display units (VDUs) *147*
Volkswagen *81*

'walk through reviews' *21ff*
waste minimisation *88ff, 98*
waste disposal *90*
   actions for every workplace *40*
waste heat recovery *65*
waste recovery *89*
water heating *62*
water saving actions for every
   workplace *139*
Watt Committee on Energy *61*
Whole Foods supermarkets *98*
Winter, Georg *142*
World Development Movement *98*
World Resources Institute *91*
World Watch Institute *40, 43, 142*
World Wide Fund for Nature *20, 120, 123*

Zweckform papers *49*